I0012110

Power Query for Business Intelligence

A Beginner's Guide

Kiet Huynh

Table of Contents

PART 1
Introduction to Power Query and Business Intelligence

1. What is Power Query?

1.1. What is Business Intelligence (BI)?

Business Intelligence (BI) is a comprehensive set of technologies, processes, and tools that enable organizations to collect, analyze, and present business information. The primary goal of BI is to transform raw data into meaningful and actionable insights, facilitating informed decision-making within an organization. BI encompasses a range of activities, including data gathering, data cleansing, data modeling, data analysis, and data visualization.

In essence, BI provides a framework for turning vast amounts of data into valuable knowledge, allowing businesses to identify trends, patterns, and opportunities. By leveraging BI, organizations can gain a competitive advantage, enhance operational efficiency, and make strategic decisions based on a deeper understanding of their data.

Key components of Business Intelligence include:

1. **Data Warehousing:** BI often involves the creation of data warehouses, centralized repositories that store and organize data from various sources. Data warehouses provide a unified view of an organization's information, making it easier to analyze and extract insights.

2. Data Analysis: BI tools enable users to analyze large datasets quickly and efficiently. This involves querying, filtering, and manipulating data to identify relevant information and trends.

3. Reporting and Dashboards: BI platforms offer reporting capabilities that allow users to create visually appealing reports and dashboards. These visual representations make it simpler for stakeholders to comprehend complex data and make data-driven decisions.

4. Data Visualization: BI emphasizes the importance of presenting data in a visually compelling manner. This includes charts, graphs, and other visualizations that help convey information in an easily understandable format.

5. Performance Monitoring: BI enables organizations to monitor key performance indicators (KPIs) and track the success of various business processes. This ongoing monitoring ensures that businesses stay agile and responsive to changes in their environment.

In summary, Business Intelligence empowers organizations to harness the power of data, fostering a culture of data-driven decision-making. It plays a crucial role in shaping strategies, improving operations, and maintaining a competitive edge in today's dynamic business landscape.

1.2. Where does Power Query fit into BI?

Power Query plays a pivotal role in the Business Intelligence (BI) landscape by serving as a robust data transformation tool within the Microsoft Power BI ecosystem. It is specifically designed to address the challenges associated with data preparation and cleansing, enabling users to seamlessly connect to various data sources, transform raw data into a structured format, and load it into BI tools for analysis and visualization.

Integration with Data Sources:

Power Query excels in its ability to connect to diverse data sources, ranging from databases and spreadsheets to online services and APIs. This versatility allows users to pull in data from multiple origin points, aggregating information for a comprehensive BI solution.

Data Transformation and Cleaning:

One of the key strengths of Power Query lies in its data transformation capabilities. It allows users to reshape, clean, and combine data from different sources, ensuring that the information is standardized and ready for analysis. This transformation process is crucial for BI initiatives, as it ensures the data is accurate, consistent, and suitable for reporting.

Data Modeling and Enrichment:

Within the BI framework, Power Query facilitates data modeling and enrichment. Users can create relationships between tables, define calculated columns, and enrich the dataset with additional information. This step is vital for creating a solid foundation for analytics and generating meaningful insights.

Seamless Integration with Power BI:

Power Query seamlessly integrates with Power BI, Microsoft's BI visualization tool. The transformed and enriched data can be loaded directly into Power BI for further analysis and visualization. This integration ensures a smooth workflow, allowing users to transition seamlessly from data preparation to creating insightful reports and dashboards.

Automation and Reusability:

Power Query supports automation, enabling users to create reusable queries that automatically update when the source data changes. This feature streamlines the data preparation process and ensures that BI reports remain up-to-date with the latest information.

In summary, Power Query serves as the linchpin between raw data and actionable insights within the BI ecosystem. Its capabilities in connecting to diverse data sources, transforming and cleaning data, and integrating seamlessly with BI visualization tools make it an indispensable component for organizations aiming to derive value from their data for informed decision-making.

1.3. Benefits of using Power Query

Power Query offers a multitude of benefits that significantly enhance the data preparation and transformation process within the Business Intelligence (BI) realm. Here are key advantages associated with using Power Query:

1. Streamlined Data Connectivity:

Power Query provides a user-friendly interface for connecting to a wide array of data sources, including databases, spreadsheets, online services, and more. This versatility simplifies the data integration process, allowing users to easily access and consolidate data from diverse origins.

2. Data Transformation Capabilities:

Power Query empowers users to shape and transform raw data efficiently. Its intuitive interface enables the application of various transformations, such as filtering, sorting, and aggregating data. This flexibility ensures that data is prepared in a format conducive to analysis and reporting.

3. Data Cleaning and Quality Assurance:

Ensuring data accuracy and consistency is a critical aspect of BI. Power Query facilitates the cleaning of data by providing tools to handle missing values, remove duplicates, and address inconsistencies. This ensures that the data used for analysis is reliable and error-free.

4. Easier Data Enrichment:

Power Query supports data enrichment by allowing users to create relationships between tables, merge data from different sources, and incorporate calculated columns. These capabilities enhance the depth and richness of the dataset, enabling more comprehensive analysis and reporting.

5. Time Efficiency:

By automating repetitive data preparation tasks, Power Query significantly reduces the time and effort required for data cleaning and transformation. Users can create reusable queries and workflows, leading to increased efficiency and faster time-to-insight.

6. Seamless Integration with BI Tools:

Power Query seamlessly integrates with popular BI tools like Microsoft Power BI. This integration ensures a smooth transition from data preparation to analysis and visualization, providing a cohesive end-to-end solution for BI projects.

7. Data Refresh and Updates:

Power Query supports automatic data refresh, ensuring that BI reports and dashboards remain up-to-date with the latest information. This real-time updating capability is crucial for maintaining the relevance and accuracy of BI insights.

8. User-Friendly Interface:

Designed with a user-friendly interface, Power Query is accessible to both beginners and experienced users. Its intuitive drag-and-drop functionality, combined with a formula language (M language), makes it easy for users to perform complex data transformations without extensive coding knowledge.

In summary, the benefits of using Power Query extend across the entire BI workflow, from data connectivity to preparation and integration with visualization tools. Its efficiency, flexibility, and user-friendly features make it an invaluable asset for organizations seeking to leverage their data for meaningful business insights.

2. Getting Started with Power Query

2.1. Installing and launching Power Query

Power Query is a powerful tool that seamlessly integrates with various Microsoft applications, providing an intuitive interface for data transformation and preparation. In this section, we'll walk through the process of installing and launching Power Query.

Installing Power Query:

To begin your Power Query journey, you'll first need to ensure that Power Query is installed on your system. Follow these steps:

- If you are using Microsoft Excel (2010/2013/2016/2019) or Microsoft 365, Power Query may already be included. Check for the "Data" tab in Excel to see if the "Get Data" or "Power Query" options are available.

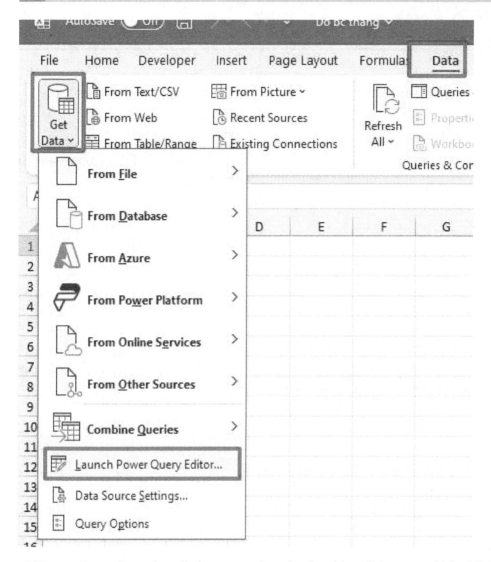

- If Power Query is not installed, you can download and install it as an add-in. Visit the official Microsoft Power Query download page, select the version compatible with your Excel or Power BI Desktop, and follow the installation instructions.

- For users of Power BI Desktop, Power Query is typically integrated by default. Ensure you have the latest version of Power BI Desktop installed to access the full range of Power Query features.

Launching Power Query:

Once Power Query is installed, launching it is a straightforward process:

- In Microsoft Excel, navigate to the "Data" tab, where you'll find the "Get Data" or "Get & Transform Data" option. Clicking on this option will open the Power Query Editor.

- In Power BI Desktop, the Power Query Editor can be accessed through the "Home" tab. Click on the "Transform data" option to open the Power Query Editor.

- Alternatively, you can launch Power Query directly from the Windows Start menu or the Power BI Desktop application.

Power Query Interface Overview:

Upon launching Power Query, you'll be greeted by the Power Query Editor Interface. Familiarizing yourself with this interface is crucial for efficient data manipulation. Key components include:

- **Ribbon:** Similar to other Microsoft applications, the Ribbon at the top provides various tabs and commands for data transformation.

- Query Pane: Located on the left, this pane displays a list of queries associated with your current workbook or data source.

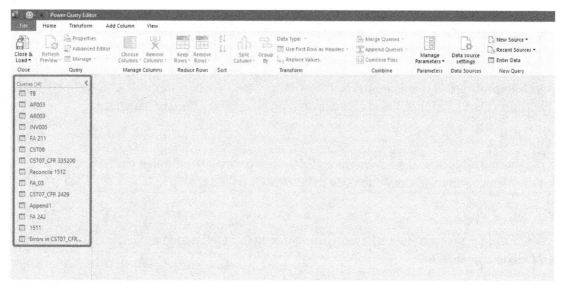

- Query Settings: On the right side, you'll find the Query Settings pane, where you can manage query properties, such as renaming and applying transformations.

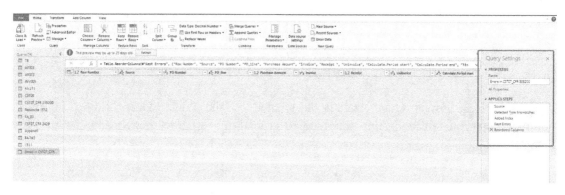

- Data Preview: The central area of the editor displays a preview of your data, allowing you to interactively apply transformations.

With Power Query installed and launched, you are now ready to delve into the exciting world of data transformation and preparation for Business Intelligence.

In the next sections, we'll explore the Power Query Editor Interface in detail and learn how to import data from different sources.

2.2. The Power Query Editor Interface

The Power Query Editor Interface serves as the command center for data transformation and manipulation. Understanding its components is crucial for users navigating through the process of preparing data for Business Intelligence. Let's explore the key elements of the Power Query Editor Interface:

1. Home Tab:

  - The Home tab is your primary workspace, offering a range of tools and commands for data transformation.

  - Here, you'll find options to access data sources, apply transformations, manage queries, and more.

  - The "Close & Apply" button, located in this tab, is used to apply the changes made in Power Query and close the editor.

2. Query Pane:

- Located on the left side of the interface, the Query Pane displays a list of all queries associated with the current workbook or data source.

- Users can navigate between queries, manage query properties, and organize their workflow from this pane.

3. Query Settings Pane:

- Positioned on the right side of the interface, the Query Settings Pane provides detailed information about the currently selected query.

- Users can rename queries, adjust properties, and manage applied steps using this pane.

4. Formula Bar:

- The Formula Bar is located at the top of the Power Query Editor, displaying the formula or expression for the currently selected step.

- Users can manually enter formulas or edit existing ones, providing a more granular control over data transformations.

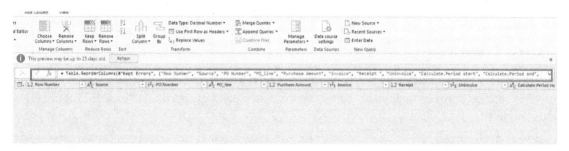

5. Data Preview:

- The central area of the Power Query Editor displays a preview of the data. This section allows users to interact with the data, visually inspect changes, and ensure the accuracy of transformations.

- Users can select columns, filter data, and perform other actions directly in the Data Preview.

6. Applied Steps:

- At the bottom of the Power Query Editor, the Applied Steps section showcases a chronological list of all transformations and actions applied to the data.

- Users can review and modify these steps, providing a transparent and traceable record of the data preparation process.

7. Query Dependencies:

- The Query Dependencies view, accessible from the View tab, displays a visual representation of relationships between queries in the workbook. This feature is particularly useful for complex data models.

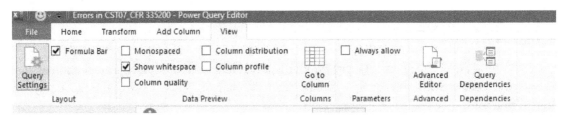

8. Advanced Editor:

- For users comfortable with the M language (Power Query's underlying language), the Advanced Editor provides a text-based interface for creating custom queries and expressions.

Understanding these components of the Power Query Editor Interface sets the foundation for efficient data preparation. In the next section, we will explore the practical aspects of importing data from various sources, demonstrating the versatility of Power Query in handling diverse datasets.

2.3. Importing data from different sources

Power Query offers a versatile platform for importing data from a variety of sources, enabling users to seamlessly integrate and transform data for Business Intelligence purposes. This section provides a step-by-step guide on how to import data from different sources using Power Query.

Step-by-Step Guide:

1. Open Power BI Desktop:

- Launch Power BI Desktop on your computer.

2. Go to "Home" Tab:

- In the Power BI Desktop interface, navigate to the "Home" tab.

3. Click on "Get Data":

- Click on the "Get Data" option in the "Home" tab. A dropdown menu will appear with various data source options.

4. Select a Data Source:

- Choose the appropriate data source from the list. Power Query supports a wide range of sources, including Excel, CSV, databases (SQL Server, Oracle, MySQL), SharePoint, Web, and more.

5. Provide Connection Details:

- Depending on the selected data source, a dialog box will appear prompting you to provide connection details. This may include file paths, server addresses, credentials, etc.

- For example, when connecting to a database, you would need to enter server details, database name, and authentication credentials.

6. Preview and Transform Data:

- After providing connection details, Power Query will connect to the selected data source and display a preview of the data in the Power Query Editor.

- Use the Power Query Editor to preview and apply transformations to the data before importing it into Power BI.

7. Transform and Cleanse Data (Optional):

- Utilize the Power Query Editor tools to transform and cleanse the data as needed. This may involve filtering rows, removing duplicates, renaming columns, or applying other data manipulation operations.

8. Click "Close & Apply":

- Once satisfied with the data preview and any applied transformations, click "Close & Apply" in the Power Query Editor to import the data into Power BI.

9. Review Imported Data:

- The imported data will now be available in the Power BI Desktop, ready for use in creating reports and visualizations.

- You can view the imported tables in the "Fields" pane on the right side of the Power BI Desktop interface.

10. Refresh Data (Optional):

- If your data source is dynamic and regularly updated, you can set up automatic refresh options in Power BI to ensure that your reports reflect the latest data.

By following these steps, users can effectively import data from various sources into Power BI using Power Query. This flexibility in data connectivity is a key feature that empowers users to harness diverse datasets for Business Intelligence and reporting purposes.

3. Data Sources and Connectivity

3.1. Connecting to common data sources (e.g., Excel, CSV, databases)

Power Query excels in its ability to seamlessly connect to a variety of data sources, offering users flexibility in importing and transforming data. In this section, we'll explore step-by-step instructions on connecting to common data sources such as Excel, CSV files, and databases.

Connecting to Excel:

1. Open Power Query Editor:

  - Launch Power Query from the "Data" tab in Excel by selecting "Get Data" or "Get & Transform Data."

2. Choose Excel as a Data Source:

  - In the Power Query Editor, click on "Home" and select "Excel" from the "Get Data" menu.

3. Select the Excel File:

  - Browse and choose the Excel file you want to import. Click "Import" to proceed.

4. Navigate through Data Import Wizard:

  - A data import wizard will appear, allowing you to preview and select specific sheets or tables for import. Follow the wizard to define import settings.

5. Transform and Load Data:

  - After selecting the desired data, you can apply transformations if needed. Once satisfied, click "Close & Apply" to load the data into Power Query.

Connecting to CSV Files:

1. Open Power Query Editor:

- Launch Power Query Editor in Excel or Power BI Desktop.

2. Choose CSV as a Data Source:

- In the Power Query Editor, click on "Home" and select "Text/CSV" from the "Get Data" menu.

3. Select the CSV File:

- Navigate to and select the CSV file you wish to import. Click "Import" to proceed.

4. Configure Import Settings:

- The data import wizard will appear, allowing you to preview and adjust settings like delimiter, encoding, and data types. Make necessary configurations and proceed.

5. Transform and Load Data:

- Apply any required transformations, then click "Close & Apply" to load the data into Power Query.

Connecting to Databases:

1. Open Power Query Editor:

- Launch Power Query Editor.

2. Choose Database as a Data Source:

- Click on "Home" and select the database type (e.g., SQL Server, MySQL) from the "Get Data" menu.

3. Configure Database Connection:

- Provide necessary connection details such as server name, database name, and authentication credentials. Click "OK" to establish the connection.

4. Navigate Database Objects:

- A navigator will appear, displaying available tables or views. Select the desired objects for import.

5. Transform and Load Data:

- Apply transformations if needed and click "Close & Apply" to load the data into Power Query.

By following these steps, users can effortlessly connect Power Query to common data sources, ensuring a smooth data import process for subsequent analysis and transformation.

3.2. Understanding data types and formatting

In Power Query, comprehending data types and formatting is essential for accurate data manipulation and analysis. This section provides an in-depth exploration of how Power Query handles data types, the importance of understanding them, and how to manage formatting effectively.

Data Types in Power Query:

1. Automatic Detection:

- Power Query automatically detects data types when importing from various sources. This includes recognizing numbers, text, dates, and other data formats.

2. Data Type Icons:

- In the Power Query Editor, each column is assigned a data type icon. Understanding these icons is crucial for assessing the nature of the data in a column. For instance, a calendar icon indicates a date data type, while an "ABC" icon denotes text.

3. Changing Data Types:

- Users can manually change data types by selecting a column, right-clicking, and choosing the desired data type from the context menu. This ensures that data is interpreted correctly during subsequent transformations.

Formatting Data:

1. Text and Number Formatting:

- Power Query allows users to apply formatting to text and number columns. This includes options for specifying the number of decimal places, adding currency symbols, or formatting dates.

2. Date and Time Formatting:

- Understanding date and time formats is crucial. Power Query provides functions to format date and time columns according to specific requirements, ensuring consistency in representation.

3. Locale Settings:

- Power Query considers locale settings during data import. It adapts to the regional format for numbers, dates, and times. Users should be aware of these settings to maintain consistency in data interpretation.

Dealing with Data Type Mismatches:

1. Data Type Errors:

- Mismatches in data types can lead to errors during data transformation. Power Query highlights such errors in the "Applied Steps" section, allowing users to identify and resolve issues.

2. Transforming Data Types:

- Use the "Change Type" option in the ribbon to transform data types systematically. This option provides a clear view of available data types, making it easy to select the appropriate type for each column.

Advanced Connection Options:

1. Locale-Specific Formats:

- When dealing with data from different locales, users can adjust locale-specific formats to ensure accurate data interpretation. This is particularly relevant when importing data with date, time, or number formats that vary across regions.

2. Custom Formats and Transformations:

- Power Query offers advanced options for customizing data formats and applying complex transformations. Users can utilize the M language to create custom functions, providing unparalleled flexibility in data manipulation.

Understanding data types and formatting in Power Query is fundamental to maintaining data accuracy and consistency throughout the BI workflow. By mastering these concepts, users can unlock the full potential of Power Query for effective data preparation and analysis.

Example 1: Automatic Detection

Consider a CSV file with a "Sales" column. Power Query detects the data type automatically, assigning a currency icon to indicate a number with a currency format.

Before Transformation:

| Sales |

| $500.25 |

| $789.50 |

| $123.75 |

After Automatic Detection:

| Sales (Number) |

| 500.25 |

| 789.50 |

| 123.75 |

Example 2: Changing Data Types

If the "Sales" column was mistakenly detected as text, you can manually change the data type. Right-click on the column, choose "Change Type," and select "Decimal Number" to correctly interpret the values.

Before Transformation:

| Sales |

| 500.25 |

| 789.50 |

| 123.75 |

After Manual Data Type Change:

| Sales (Number) |

| 500.25 |

| 789.50 |

| 123.75 |

Formatting Data:

Example 3: Text and Number Formatting

Suppose you have a column "Price" that needs specific formatting. Use the formatting options in Power Query to add a currency symbol and two decimal places.

Before Transformation:

| Price |

| 25.5 |

| 50.75 |

| 30 |

After Formatting:

| Price (Formatted) |

| $25.50 |

| $50.75 |

| $30.00 |

Example 4: Date and Time Formatting

If you're dealing with a "TransactionDate" column, you can apply a custom date format using the "Transform" options.

Before Transformation:

| TransactionDate |

| 2022-01-15 |

| 2022-02-28 |

| 2022-03-10 |

After Formatting:

| TransactionDate (Formatted) |

| 15-Jan-2022 |

| 28-Feb-2022 |

| 10-Mar-2022 |

Dealing with Data Type Mismatches:

Example 5: Transforming Data Types

Suppose a "Quantity" column was imported as text. Use the "Change Type" option to transform it into a whole number.

Before Transformation:

| Quantity |

| 100 |

| 50 |

| 75 |

After Data Type Transformation:

| Quantity (Number) |

| 100 |

| 50 |

| 75 |

These examples illustrate the practical aspects of handling data types and formatting in Power Query. Whether it's automatic detection, manual adjustments, or advanced formatting, Power Query provides a versatile environment for precise data manipulation.

3.3. Advanced connection options

In Power Query, advanced connection options provide users with enhanced capabilities for accessing, transforming, and combining data from diverse sources. This section delves into advanced features that empower users to optimize their data connectivity and extraction processes.

1. Custom Queries and SQL Statements:

- Power Query allows users to input custom queries and SQL statements when connecting to databases. This advanced option is valuable for executing specific database queries that go beyond standard import options.

Example: Connecting to a SQL Server with a Custom Query

SELECT CustomerID, FirstName, LastName

FROM Customers

WHERE Country = 'USA'

2. Query Folding:

- Query folding is a performance optimization technique that pushes certain data transformations back to the data source, reducing the amount of data brought into Power Query for processing. It is particularly useful for databases that support query folding, as it can significantly enhance performance.

Example: Leveraging Query Folding for Date Filtering

= Table.SelectColumns(Source, {"OrderID", "Product", "Quantity", "OrderDate"})

   => Table.FilterRows(#"Removed Other Columns", each [OrderDate] >= #datetime(2022, 01, 01))

3. Merging Queries from Different Sources:

- Advanced connection options in Power Query enable users to merge data from various sources into a single query. This feature is beneficial when dealing with data spread across multiple files or databases that need consolidation.

Example: Merging Customer Data from Excel and SQL Server

ExcelData = Excel.Workbook(File.Contents("C:\Path\To\Excel\File.xlsx")),

SQLData = Sql.Database("serverName", "databaseName"),

MergedData = Table.NestedJoin(ExcelData, {"CustomerID"}, SQLData, {"CustomerID"}, "MergedData")

4. Web Data Connector:

- Power Query supports Web Data Connector (WDC), allowing users to connect to web-based data sources by creating custom connectors. This is particularly useful for integrating data from online APIs and services directly into Power Query.

Example: Creating a Web Data Connector for Financial Data

```
let

  Source = Web.Contents("https://api.example.com/financial-data"),

  Json = Json.Document(Source),

  FinancialData = Json[Data]

in

  FinancialData
```

5. Folder and File Browsing:

- Power Query's ability to connect to folders and browse through files provides a dynamic way to import data from multiple files within a directory. Users can apply transformations to all files in a folder, streamlining the process of working with large datasets.

Example: Loading Data from Multiple CSV Files in a Folder

FolderPath = "C:\Path\To\CSV\Files",

Source = Folder.Files(FolderPath),

CombinedData = Table.Combine(List.Transform(Source[Content], each Csv.Document(Csv.FromText(_))))

By leveraging these advanced connection options, users can harness the full potential of Power Query, extending their capabilities to handle complex data scenarios and ensuring a more efficient and customized data preparation process for Business Intelligence.

4. Data Cleansing and Transformation

4.1. Filtering and removing unwanted data

In the realm of Power Query, data cleansing is a fundamental step in preparing datasets for Business Intelligence. Filtering and removing unwanted data allow users to refine their datasets, ensuring that only relevant and essential information is retained. This section outlines specific techniques and procedures for effective data filtering and removal.

Filtering Data:

1. Basic Filtering:

- Power Query provides a user-friendly interface for basic filtering. Users can easily filter columns based on specific criteria, such as numeric ranges, text values, or date ranges.

Example: Filtering Rows with Sales Greater Than 100

= Table.SelectRows(Source, each [Sales] > 100)

2. Text Filters:

- Users can apply text filters to columns, allowing for operations like starts with, contains, ends with, or custom text patterns. This is particularly useful for cleaning and standardizing textual data.

Example: Filtering Products Containing "Widget" in the Name

= Table.SelectRows(Source, each Text.Contains([ProductName], "Widget"))

3. Date and Time Filters:

- Filtering data based on date and time criteria is essential. Power Query provides options for filtering data before or after specific dates, within date ranges, or based on custom date functions.

Example: Filtering Orders Placed After January 1, 2022

= Table.SelectRows(Source, each [OrderDate] >= #datetime(2022, 01, 01))

Removing Unwanted Data:

1. Removing Duplicates:

- Duplicate data can skew analysis results. Power Query enables users to identify and remove duplicate rows based on selected columns, ensuring data integrity.

Example: Removing Duplicates Based on CustomerID

= Table.Distinct(Source, {"CustomerID"})

2. Filtering Null or Blank Values:

- Filtering out rows with null or blank values is crucial for data quality. Power Query allows users to easily exclude rows where specific columns have missing or empty data.

Example: Removing Rows with Null Values in the ProductName Column

= Table.SelectRows(Source, each [ProductName] <> null)

3. Advanced Filtering and Custom Functions:

- Advanced filtering techniques involve the use of custom functions written in the M language. This allows users to implement complex filtering logic tailored to their specific data cleansing needs.

Example: Filtering Rows Based on a Custom Function

= Table.SelectRows(Source, each CustomFunction([Column1], [Column2]))

By mastering these filtering and removal techniques, users can effectively streamline their datasets, eliminating unnecessary or duplicate information. This sets the stage for further transformations and analysis in the Business Intelligence process.

In this section, we'll walk through specific examples to illustrate how to use Power Query for filtering and removing unwanted data.

Example 1: Basic Numeric Filtering

Suppose we have a dataset with a "Sales" column, and we want to filter out rows where sales are less than or equal to 100.

Before Transformation:

Product	Sales
A	120
B	90
C	150

After Basic Numeric Filtering:

= Table.SelectRows(Source, each [Sales] > 100)

Product	Sales
A	120
C	150

Example 2: Text Filtering

Assume we have a "ProductType" column, and we want to filter rows where the product type contains the word "Electronics."

Before Transformation:

Product	ProductType
Laptop	Electronics
Headphones	Audio Electronics
Shirt	Apparel

After Text Filtering:

= Table.SelectRows(Source, each Text.Contains([ProductType], "Electronics"))

Product	ProductType
Laptop	Electronics
Headphones	Audio Electronics

Example 3: Date Filtering

Suppose we have an "OrderDate" column, and we want to filter out rows where orders were placed before January 1, 2022.

Before Transformation:

OrderID	OrderDate
101	2021-12-20
102	2022-01-05
103	2022-02-10

After Date Filtering:

= Table.SelectRows(Source, each [OrderDate] >= #datetime(2022, 01, 01))

OrderID	OrderDate
102	2022-01-05
103	2022-02-10

Example 4: Removing Duplicates

Assume we have a dataset with duplicate entries based on the "CustomerID" column.

Before Transformation:

CustomerID	Name
001	Alice
002	Bob
001	Alice

After Removing Duplicates:

= Table.Distinct(Source, {"CustomerID"})

CustomerID	Name
001	Alice
002	Bob

These examples showcase how Power Query can be used to filter and remove unwanted data based on various criteria, providing a clean and refined dataset for subsequent Business Intelligence activities.

4.2. Renaming and formatting columns

Renaming and formatting columns in Power Query are essential steps in the data cleansing and transformation process. This section details the techniques and procedures for effectively renaming columns and applying formatting to ensure consistency and clarity in the dataset.

Renaming Columns:

1. Basic Renaming:

- Power Query allows users to easily rename columns using a straightforward approach. Select the column, right-click, and choose "Rename" to input the desired name.

Example: Renaming the "ProductID" Column to "ID"

= Table.RenameColumns(Source,{{"ProductID", "ID"}})

2. Batch Renaming:

- For scenarios where multiple columns need renaming, Power Query supports batch renaming. Users can provide a list of old and new column names for efficient renaming.

Example: Renaming Multiple Columns Simultaneously

= Table.RenameColumns(Source,{{"OldColumn1", "NewColumn1"}, {"OldColumn2", "NewColumn2"}})

3. Using the Advanced Editor for Renaming:

- Advanced users comfortable with the M language can utilize the Advanced Editor for more complex renaming tasks. This allows for custom renaming logic using the RenameColumns function.

Example: Custom Renaming Logic in Advanced Editor

= Table.RenameColumns(Source, each [Name] & "_Renamed", {"Name"})

Formatting Columns:

1. Applying Number Formatting:

- Power Query provides options for formatting numeric columns, including setting the number of decimal places, adding a thousand separator, or applying a specific currency format.

Example: Formatting the "Revenue" Column as Currency

= Table.TransformColumns(Source, {{"Revenue", Currency.From}})

2. Date and Time Formatting:

- Ensure consistency in date and time representations by applying specific formats. Power Query supports various date and time formats, allowing users to standardize the display.

Example: Formatting the "OrderDate" Column as Short Date

= Table.TransformColumns(Source, {{"OrderDate", each DateTime.ToText(_, "MM/dd/yyyy"), type text}})

3. Custom Text Formatting:

- When dealing with text columns, users can apply custom formatting to ensure consistency. This includes converting text to uppercase, lowercase, or applying specific patterns.

Example: Converting "ProductName" to Uppercase

= Table.TransformColumns(Source, {{"ProductName", Text.Upper}})

4. Conditional Formatting:

- Advanced users can implement conditional formatting based on specific criteria. This allows for dynamic formatting based on the values in a column.

Example: Applying Conditional Formatting to Highlight High Sales

· = Table.AddColumn(Source, "FormattedSales", each if [Sales] > 1000 then Text.From([Sales]) & " High" else Text.From([Sales]) & " Normal")

By mastering the techniques of renaming and formatting columns in Power Query, users can ensure that their datasets are not only accurate but also presented in a consistent and user-friendly manner, laying a solid foundation for subsequent Business Intelligence tasks.

4.3. Combining and splitting columns

Combining and splitting columns in Power Query provide powerful tools for restructuring data to meet specific requirements. This section guides you through the step-by-step process of effectively combining and splitting columns for a more refined and usable dataset.

Combining Columns:

1. Basic Column Combination:

- To combine two or more columns into a single column, you can use the "Add Column" tab and select "Merge Columns." Choose the columns to combine and specify a delimiter if needed.

Example: Combining "FirstName" and "LastName" into a "FullName" Column

= Table.AddColumn(Source, "FullName", each [FirstName] & " " & [LastName])

2. Advanced Column Combination using the M language:

- For more complex column combining tasks, you can use the Advanced Editor and write custom M language expressions using the "&" operator or other concatenation functions.

Example: Custom Concatenation with a Separator in Advanced Editor

= Table.AddColumn(Source, "CombinedColumn", each Text.From([Column1]) & "_" & Text.From([Column2]))

3. Column Combination with Conditional Logic:

- You can incorporate conditional logic while combining columns. This allows you to create dynamic combined columns based on specific conditions.

Example: Combining "City" and "Country" with a Separator, Considering Empty Country

= Table.AddColumn(Source, "Location", each if [Country] <> null then [City] & ", " & [Country] else [City])

Splitting Columns:

1. Basic Column Splitting:

- To split a column into multiple columns, use the "Transform" tab and select "Split Column." Choose a delimiter or specify the number of characters for splitting.

Example: Splitting "FullName" into "FirstName" and "LastName" Columns with a Space Delimiter

= Table.SplitColumn(Source, "FullName", Splitter.SplitTextByDelimiter(" ", QuoteStyle.Csv), {"FirstName", "LastName"})

2. Advanced Column Splitting with the M language:

- For more control over column splitting, especially when dealing with complex delimiters, use the Advanced Editor to write custom M language expressions using functions like Text.Split.

Example: Custom Splitting with a Specific Delimiter in Advanced Editor

= Table.SplitColumn(Source, "CombinedColumn", Splitter.SplitTextByDelimiter("_", QuoteStyle.Csv), {"Part1", "Part2"})

3. Column Splitting based on Position or Number of Characters:

- You can split a column based on the position of characters or a specified number of characters. This is helpful when dealing with fixed-width data.

Example: Splitting "PostalCode" into "AreaCode" and "LocalCode" Based on Character Position

= Table.SplitColumn(Source, "PostalCode", Splitter.SplitTextByPositions({0, 3}, false), {"AreaCode", "LocalCode"})

Combining and Splitting Multiple Columns:

1. Combining Multiple Columns into One:

- When dealing with multiple columns to be combined, create a custom column that concatenates the values from several columns.

Example: Combining "Address," "City," and "Country" into a Single "FullAddress" Column

= Table.AddColumn(Source, "FullAddress", each [Address] & ", " & [City] & ", " & [Country])

2. Splitting a Column into Multiple Columns:

- To split a single column into multiple columns, use the "Transform" tab and select "Split Column" with the desired delimiter.

Example: Splitting "MultipleValues" into Separate Columns Based on a Comma Delimiter

= Table.SplitColumn(Source, "MultipleValues", Splitter.SplitTextByDelimiter(",", QuoteStyle.Csv), {"Value1", "Value2", "Value3"})

By mastering the techniques of combining and splitting columns in Power Query, you gain the ability to reshape and structure your data according to your specific needs, ensuring a more efficient and tailored approach to data cleansing and transformation.

Scenarios for Using Column Combining and Splitting in Power Query:

1. Combining First Name and Last Name:

- **Scenario:** When your dataset has separate columns for first names and last names, and you want to create a single column for full names.

- **Solution:**

   = Table.AddColumn(Source, "FullName", each [FirstName] & " " & [LastName])

2. Creating a Unique Identifier from Multiple Columns:

- **Scenario:** Combining multiple columns to create a unique identifier or key for each record in the dataset.

- **Solution:**

   = Table.AddColumn(Source, "UniqueID", each [Prefix] & "-" & Text.From([ID]))

3. Splitting Full Address into Components:

- **Scenario:** When dealing with a "FullAddress" column and you need separate columns for street address, city, and country.

- **Solution:**

```
= Table.SplitColumn(Source, "FullAddress", Splitter.SplitTextByDelimiter(", ", QuoteStyle.Csv), {"StreetAddress", "City", "Country"})
```

4. Extracting Information from Combined Columns:

- **Scenario:** Extracting specific information from a combined column, such as splitting a "ProductCode" into category and code.

- **Solution:**

```
= Table.SplitColumn(Source, "ProductCode", Splitter.SplitTextByDelimiter("-", QuoteStyle.Csv), {"Category", "Code"})
```

5. Handling Multiple Values in a Single Column:

- **Scenario:** Dealing with a column containing multiple values separated by a delimiter, and you need to split them into separate columns.

- **Solution:**

```
= Table.SplitColumn(Source, "MultipleValues", Splitter.SplitTextByDelimiter(",", QuoteStyle.Csv), {"Value1", "Value2", "Value3"})
```

6. Formatting Phone Numbers or Postal Codes:

- **Scenario:** Combining or splitting columns to format data such as phone numbers or postal codes for consistency.

- **Solution:**

```
= Table.TransformColumns(Source, {{"PhoneNumber", PhoneNumber.FromText}})
```

7. Handling Concatenated Columns with Custom Logic:

- **Scenario:** Combining columns with custom logic or adding a separator between values.

- **Solution:**

  = Table.AddColumn(Source, "CombinedColumn", each Text.From([Column1]) & "_" & Text.From([Column2]))

8. Dealing with Fixed-Width Data:

- **Scenario:** Splitting a column based on fixed-width positions in cases where the data follows a structured, fixed-width format.

- **Solution:**

  = Table.SplitColumn(Source, "FixedWidthColumn", Splitter.SplitTextByPositions({0, 5, 10}, false), {"Part1", "Part2", "Part3"})

These scenarios demonstrate the versatility of column combining and splitting in Power Query, allowing users to adapt their datasets to specific requirements, clean and structure data effectively, and prepare it for further analysis in a Business Intelligence context.

Scenario: Combining First Name and Last Name

Step-by-Step Guide:

1. Open Power Query Editor:

- Load your dataset into Power Query Editor by selecting the relevant data source, such as an Excel file or a database.

2. Identify Columns:

- Identify the columns containing first names ("FirstName") and last names ("LastName") that you want to combine.

3. Navigate to "Add Column" Tab:

- In the Power Query Editor, go to the "Add Column" tab.

4. Select "Custom Column":

- Click on "Custom Column" to create a new column with a custom formula.

5. Enter Formula:

- In the "Custom Column" dialog, enter a name for the new column, for example, "FullName."

- Enter the formula using the "&" operator to concatenate the first name and last name:

```m
[FirstName] & " " & [LastName]
```

6. Click "OK":

- Click "OK" to close the dialog and create the new column.

7. Review and Apply:

- Review the changes in the Power Query preview. Ensure that the "FullName" column is created as expected.

8. Click "Close & Apply":

- Once satisfied with the changes, click "Close & Apply" to apply the transformations and close the Power Query Editor.

Scenario: Splitting Full Address into Components

Step-by-Step Guide:

1. Open Power Query Editor:

- Load your dataset into Power Query Editor.

2. Identify Column:

- Identify the column containing the full address ("FullAddress") that you want to split into components.

3. Navigate to "Transform" Tab:

- In the Power Query Editor, go to the "Transform" tab.

4. Select "Split Column":

- Click on "Split Column" and choose "By Delimiter" since the full address likely has components separated by a delimiter.

5. Specify Delimiter:

- Specify the delimiter (e.g., ", ") used in the full address.

6. Choose New Column Names:

- Choose names for the new columns that will store the split components, such as "StreetAddress," "City," and "Country."

7. Click "OK":

- Click "OK" to apply the splitting transformation.

8. Review and Apply:

- Review the changes in the Power Query preview. Ensure that the new columns are created with the split components.

9. Click "Close & Apply":

- Once satisfied with the changes, click "Close & Apply" to apply the transformations and close the Power Query Editor.

By following these step-by-step guides, you can efficiently combine or split columns in Power Query to structure your data according to your specific needs.

5. Data Modeling and Aggregation

5.1. Creating relationships between tables

In the realm of business intelligence, creating relationships between tables is a fundamental step towards unlocking the full potential of your data. Power Query provides a robust framework for establishing connections between different tables, allowing you to harness the collective insights residing in disparate datasets. Let's delve into the intricacies of this crucial process:

Understanding Table Relationships:

Before embarking on the journey of creating relationships, it's imperative to comprehend the nature of your data. Identify key fields that serve as common denominators between tables. These fields, often referred to as keys, are the linchpin for establishing relationships. Whether it's a unique identifier or a shared attribute, selecting the right keys is pivotal for accurate and meaningful associations.

Steps to Create Relationships:

1. Open Power Query Editor: Begin by navigating to the Power Query Editor, the workspace where you sculpt and refine your data transformations.

2. Load Tables: Import the tables you intend to connect. Tables may represent different aspects of your business, such as sales, customers, or products.

3. Identify Key Columns: Examine each table and pinpoint the columns that will serve as the basis for your relationships. These columns should contain comparable values across tables.

4. Access the Relationship View: Power Query facilitates relationship creation through an intuitive Relationship View. Access this view to visualize existing relationships and forge new connections.

5. Create a New Relationship: Select the key columns in the respective tables and initiate the relationship creation process. Power Query will intelligently recognize matching values, laying the groundwork for seamless data integration.

Types of Relationships:

Understanding the types of relationships is essential for optimizing data modeling. Power Query supports various relationship types, including one-to-one, one-to-many, and many-to-many. Each type caters to specific scenarios, influencing how data is consolidated and analyzed.

Managing Relationships:

Once relationships are established, it's crucial to manage and maintain them effectively. Power Query equips users with tools to modify, delete, or create additional relationships as the need arises. Regularly auditing and refining relationships ensures data accuracy and relevancy.

Creating relationships between tables is a pivotal skill in the business intelligence landscape, forming the bedrock for advanced analytics and informed decision-making. Mastering this aspect of Power Query empowers users to unlock the true potential of their data, fostering a deeper understanding of business dynamics.

5.2. Summarizing data using aggregations (e.g., sum, average, count)

Once relationships between tables are established, the next critical step in the journey of data modeling and business intelligence is the art of data summarization through aggregations. This process involves condensing large datasets into meaningful insights by applying functions such as sum, average, count, and more. Let's delve into the intricacies of data summarization:

Understanding Aggregations:

Aggregations are mathematical operations applied to groups of data to derive consolidated results. Common aggregation functions include:

- **Sum:** Adds up the values within a column.

- **Average:** Calculates the mean of a set of values.

- **Count:** Tallies the number of entries in a column.

- **Min/Max:** Determines the smallest or largest value in a set, respectively.

Applying Aggregations in Power Query:

Power Query provides a user-friendly interface to apply aggregations seamlessly. Here are the key steps:

1. Select Columns: Choose the columns containing the data you want to aggregate.

2. Access Transformations: Navigate to the Transformations tab and explore the myriad of aggregation options available.

3. Choose Aggregation Type: Depending on your analytical objectives, select the appropriate aggregation function. For instance, if analyzing sales data, summing the revenue column provides a valuable total.

4. Review Results: Power Query dynamically previews the results of your aggregations, allowing you to validate the accuracy before finalizing the transformation.

Grouping Data for Aggregation:

Effective aggregation often involves grouping data based on specific criteria. Power Query facilitates this process through the grouping functionality. Grouping allows you to categorize data based on one or more columns, creating subsets for targeted aggregations.

Utilizing Aggregations in Data Modeling:

Aggregated data plays a pivotal role in constructing robust data models for business intelligence. By summarizing information, you gain a higher-level perspective, enabling easier interpretation and decision-making. Aggregations serve as the building blocks for metrics, KPIs, and comprehensive dashboards.

Optimizing Performance:

While aggregations enhance analytical capabilities, it's crucial to consider performance optimization. Power Query provides tools to streamline and accelerate the aggregation process, ensuring that even with vast datasets, your analyses remain swift and responsive.

Mastering the art of summarizing data through aggregations empowers business analysts and intelligence professionals to distill complex information into actionable insights, laying the groundwork for informed decision-making and strategic planning.

Certainly! Let's provide more clarity on the section about "Types of Relationships":

Types of Relationships:

Establishing relationships between tables in Power Query involves defining the nature of the connection and the cardinality between the tables. The types of relationships supported in Power Query are essential for shaping how data is consolidated and analyzed. Here are the key types of relationships:

1. One-to-One Relationship:

- **Definition:** A one-to-one relationship exists when each record in the first table corresponds to exactly one record in the second table, and vice versa.

- **Use Case:** Suitable when there is a unique, singular match between records in both tables. For example, connecting a table of employees with a table of employee IDs.

2. One-to-Many Relationship:

- **Definition:** In a one-to-many relationship, each record in the first table can be associated with multiple records in the second table, but each record in the second table is linked to only one record in the first table.

- **Use Case:** Commonly used when dealing with hierarchical data, such as connecting a table of customers with a table of their orders.

3. Many-to-One Relationship:

- **Definition:** The reverse of a one-to-many relationship, where multiple records in the first table are associated with a single record in the second table.

- **Use Case:** Can be relevant when aggregating data, like connecting a table of sales transactions to a table of products.

4. Many-to-Many Relationship:

- **Definition:** A many-to-many relationship signifies that each record in both tables can be related to multiple records in the other table.

- **Use Case:** Typically resolved through an intermediary table, which is also known as a junction or link table. This relationship is useful when dealing with complex scenarios like connecting students to courses.

Understanding the nuances of these relationship types is pivotal for designing a robust data model. The choice of relationship type depends on the structure of your data and the analytical insights you aim to derive. Power Query provides the flexibility to manage and manipulate these relationships, ensuring that your data connections align with the intricacies of your business logic.

5.3. Building a data model for analysis

The culmination of creating relationships between tables and summarizing data through aggregations lies in the construction of a comprehensive data model. A well-crafted data model is the cornerstone of effective business intelligence, providing a structured framework for in-depth analysis. In this section, we explore the key steps and considerations for building a robust data model:

Understanding Data Modeling:

Data modeling is the process of organizing and structuring data to facilitate analysis and reporting. It involves defining relationships, establishing hierarchies, and shaping the data into a format that aligns with business objectives. Power Query, as a formidable tool in data modeling, empowers users to transform raw data into a cohesive and insightful model.

Key Steps in Building a Data Model:

1. Define Business Requirements:

- Before embarking on data modeling, clearly define the business requirements and objectives. Understand the questions the data model should answer and the insights stakeholders seek to gain.

2. Review Existing Relationships:

- Evaluate the relationships created between tables in Power Query. Ensure they accurately represent the real-world connections between different aspects of your business.

3. Refine Data Types and Formats:

- Standardize data types and formats across tables to ensure consistency. This step enhances the accuracy of calculations and simplifies the analysis process.

4. Create Calculated Columns and Measures:

- Leverage Power Query's capabilities to create calculated columns and measures. These dynamic elements enhance the data model by introducing customized calculations, key performance indicators (KPIs), and metrics tailored to specific business needs.

5. Utilize Hierarchies:

- Hierarchies provide a structured way to organize and drill down into data. Establish hierarchies based on the natural flow of business operations, facilitating intuitive navigation and analysis.

6. Optimize for Performance:

- Consider the performance implications of the data model. Implement optimization techniques, such as summarizing data at appropriate levels and managing relationships efficiently, to ensure swift responsiveness during analysis.

Visualization and Reporting:

A well-constructed data model sets the stage for compelling visualizations and insightful reporting. Power Query seamlessly integrates with visualization tools, allowing users to create dashboards and reports that convey meaningful information derived from the intricacies of the data model.

Iterative Refinement:

Building a data model is an iterative process. Regularly revisit and refine the model based on evolving business requirements, feedback from stakeholders, and changes in the data landscape. This iterative approach ensures that the data model remains dynamic and continues to meet the evolving needs of the business.

In conclusion, building a data model with Power Query is a transformative journey from raw data to actionable insights. By understanding business requirements, refining relationships, and optimizing for performance, users can unlock the full potential of their data, paving the way for informed decision-making and strategic planning.

6. Introduction to M Language

6.1. The syntax of the M language

The M language, at the heart of Power Query, serves as the backbone for transforming and shaping data within the Power Query Editor. Understanding the syntax of the M language is pivotal for users seeking to unlock the full potential of data manipulation. In this section, we delve into the key components of M language syntax:

Elements of M Language Syntax:

1. Case Sensitivity:

  - M language is case-sensitive. This means that uppercase and lowercase letters are treated as distinct, impacting the accuracy of your formulas. It is essential to be mindful of letter casing when writing M expressions.

2. Expressions and Statements:

  - M language is built on expressions and statements. Expressions are units of code that produce a value, while statements are complete instructions or commands. A clear distinction between the two is crucial for constructing effective M formulas.

3. Functions and Identifiers:

  - Functions play a central role in M language syntax. They are invoked to perform specific operations on data. Identifiers, on the other hand, are names given to variables, tables, or columns. Accurate usage of functions and identifiers is fundamental to crafting functional M formulas.

4. Data Types:

- M language supports various data types, including text, numbers, dates, and lists. Understanding how M handles different data types is crucial for writing formulas that manipulate and transform data accurately.

5. Operators:

- M language employs operators for performing arithmetic, logical, and comparison operations. Familiarity with operators such as +, -, , /, &&, ||, =, and <> is essential for building complex and effective M formulas.

6. Comments:

- Comments are annotations within the M code that are not executed. They serve as a valuable tool for documenting code and making it more comprehensible. Comments in M language start with "//" for single-line comments and "/" to begin a block comment, with "/" to end it.

Example M Language Formula:

Let's explore a basic example of M language syntax to illustrate its components:

```
// This is a comment
let
    // Define a variable
    Source = Excel.CurrentWorkbook(),

    // Transform data using a function
    #"Filtered Rows" = Table.SelectRows(Source, each [Sales] > 1000),

    // Add a custom column with an expression
```

```
    #"Custom Column" = Table.AddColumn(#"Filtered Rows", "Profit Margin", each [Profit] /
[Sales])

in

    // Output the final result

    #"Custom Column"
```

This example showcases the basic structure of an M formula, incorporating comments, functions, variables, and expressions.

Mastering M Language Syntax:

Becoming proficient in M language syntax requires practice and experimentation. As users navigate through the intricacies of data manipulation, a solid understanding of M syntax empowers them to construct powerful and efficient formulas within the Power Query Editor. In subsequent sections, we will delve deeper into writing M formulas for data manipulation and utilizing tools like the Formula Bar and IntelliSense.

Let's provide a concrete example of the M language syntax for better illustration:

Example M Language Formula:

Suppose we have a dataset containing information about products, including their names, prices, and quantities sold. We want to create a new column that calculates the total revenue for each product, and then filter the dataset to include only those products with revenue greater than a certain threshold.

```
// This is a comment
```

```
let
    // Define a variable named 'Source' to reference the initial dataset

    Source = Excel.CurrentWorkbook(){[Name="Products"]}[Content],


    // Add a custom column 'TotalRevenue' using the 'Add Custom Column' function

    // This column multiplies the 'Price' and 'QuantitySold' columns to calculate revenue for each product

    #"Added Custom" = Table.AddColumn(Source, "TotalRevenue", each [Price] [QuantitySold]),


    // Filter the dataset to include only rows where 'TotalRevenue' is greater than 1000

    #"Filtered Rows" = Table.SelectRows(#"Added Custom", each [TotalRevenue] > 1000)
in
    // Output the final result

    #"Filtered Rows"
```

Explanation:

1. Variable Definition (`let`):

- We start by defining a variable named `Source`, which references the initial dataset (assumed to be a table named "Products" in the current workbook).

2. Adding a Custom Column:

- We use the `Table.AddColumn` function to create a new column named "TotalRevenue." The expression within the `each` keyword calculates the total revenue for each product by multiplying the values in the "Price" and "QuantitySold" columns.

3. Filtering Rows:

- The `Table.SelectRows` function is then applied to filter the dataset. It keeps only the rows where the newly created "TotalRevenue" column is greater than 1000.

4. Final Output:

- The result is stored in the variable `#"Filtered Rows,"` representing the filtered dataset, and is the final output of our M language formula.

This example demonstrates key aspects of M language syntax, including variable definition, function usage (`Table.AddColumn` and `Table.SelectRows`), the creation of a custom column, and the application of a filter condition. Understanding and manipulating M language syntax in this manner allows users to perform complex data transformations with precision in the Power Query Editor.

6.2. Writing basic M formulas for data manipulation

Now that we've gained an understanding of the syntax of the M language, let's delve into the practical aspect of writing basic M formulas for data manipulation within the Power Query Editor. In this section, we will explore fundamental M language formulas and their application in transforming and shaping data:

Basic M Formulas:

1. Creating Custom Columns:

- One of the fundamental operations in M language is creating custom columns. This is achieved using the `Table.AddColumn` function. For instance:

// Adding a custom column named 'Total' that sums two existing columns

#"Added Custom" = Table.AddColumn(Source, "Total", each [Column1] + [Column2])

2. Filtering Rows:

- Filtering rows based on a condition is accomplished using the `Table.SelectRows` function. For example:

// Filtering rows where 'Sales' column is greater than 1000

#"Filtered Rows" = Table.SelectRows(Source, each [Sales] > 1000)

3. Renaming Columns:

- The `Table.RenameColumns` function is employed to rename columns:

// Renaming the 'OldName' column to 'NewName'

#"Renamed Columns" = Table.RenameColumns(Source, {{"OldName", "NewName"}})

4. Removing Columns:

- To eliminate unnecessary columns, use the `Table.RemoveColumns` function:

// Removing the 'UnwantedColumn'

#"Removed Columns" = Table.RemoveColumns(Source, {"UnwantedColumn"})

5. Conditional Columns:

- Creating columns based on a condition is accomplished with `Table.AddColumn` and an `if` statement:

// Adding a column 'Category' based on the value in the 'Price' column

#"Conditional Column" = Table.AddColumn(Source, "Category", each if [Price] > 100 then "High" else "Low")

Combining Formulas:

Often, more complex transformations involve combining multiple formulas. Here's an example combining filtering and creating a custom column:

```
// Filtering rows where 'Sales' is greater than 1000 and adding a custom column

#"Filtered Rows and Added Custom" = Table.AddColumn(Table.SelectRows(Source, each [Sales] > 1000), "ProfitMargin", each [Profit] / [Sales])
```

Testing and Iterating:

As you write M formulas, it's beneficial to use the Power Query Editor's interface, including the Formula Bar and IntelliSense, to test and iterate. This iterative approach allows for real-time validation of your formulas and ensures that your data manipulation aligns with your objectives.

By mastering these basic M formulas, users can effectively transform and manipulate data within Power Query, setting the stage for more advanced data modeling and analysis in subsequent stages of business intelligence workflows.

Certainly! Let's provide additional concrete examples to illustrate the concepts discussed in the section "6.2. Writing Basic M Formulas for Data Manipulation" in the book "Power Query for Business Intelligence: A Beginner's Guide":

Additional Examples of Basic M Formulas:

1. Creating Custom Columns:

  - Adding a custom column that concatenates values from two existing columns:

  ```
  // Adding a custom column named 'FullName' by concatenating 'FirstName' and 'LastName'

  #"Added Custom" = Table.AddColumn(Source, "FullName", each [FirstName] & " " & [LastName])
  ```

2. Filtering Rows:

- Filtering rows based on a condition involving multiple columns:

```
// Filtering rows where both 'Quantity' and 'Price' are greater than 10
#"Filtered Rows" = Table.SelectRows(Source, each [Quantity] > 10 and [Price] > 10)
```

3. Renaming Columns:

- Renaming multiple columns simultaneously:

```
// Renaming multiple columns at once
#"Renamed Columns" = Table.RenameColumns(Source,{{"OldName1", "NewName1"},
{"OldName2", "NewName2"}})
```

4. Removing Columns:

- Removing multiple unwanted columns in a single step:

```
// Removing multiple unwanted columns
#"Removed Columns" = Table.RemoveColumns(Source,{"UnwantedColumn1",
"UnwantedColumn2"})
```

5. Conditional Columns:

- Creating a column with more complex conditional logic:

```
// Adding a column 'Performance' based on multiple conditions
#"Conditional Column" = Table.AddColumn(Source, "Performance", each
    if [Sales] > 1000 and [Profit] > 500 then "High"
    else if [Sales] > 500 and [Profit] > 200 then "Medium"
```

```
    else "Low"
)
```

Combining Formulas:

Combining formulas allows for more intricate transformations. Here's an example combining conditional columns and filtering:

```
// Adding a column 'Status' based on 'Sales' and 'Profit', and then filtering rows
#"Combined Formulas" = Table.SelectRows(
    Table.AddColumn(Source, "Status", each if [Sales] > 1000 and [Profit] > 500 then "High" else "Low"),
    each [Status] = "High"
)
```

These examples showcase how to apply basic M formulas for various data manipulation tasks. As you experiment and gain familiarity with these formulas, you'll be better equipped to handle diverse data scenarios in your business intelligence projects using Power Query.

6.3. Using the Formula Bar and IntelliSense

In the realm of Power Query and the M language, navigating the Formula Bar and leveraging IntelliSense are indispensable skills for enhancing efficiency and accuracy in writing and editing M formulas. In this section, we will explore the functionalities of the Formula Bar and IntelliSense, providing insights into how these tools can streamline the M language coding process.

The Formula Bar:

The Formula Bar is a dedicated space within the Power Query Editor where users input and edit M formulas. It serves as the canvas for crafting data transformations and is equipped with features that facilitate a seamless coding experience.

1. Syntax Highlighting:

- The Formula Bar employs syntax highlighting, providing visual cues through color differentiation for different elements such as keywords, functions, and variables. This feature enhances code readability and helps identify potential errors.

2. Autocomplete Suggestions:

- As users type in the Formula Bar, autocomplete suggestions are dynamically provided. This not only accelerates the coding process but also reduces the likelihood of syntax errors. Pressing "Tab" or "Enter" accepts the suggested option.

3. Function Descriptions:

- Hovering over a function or keyword in the Formula Bar triggers a tooltip that displays a brief description of the selected element. This quick reference aids users in understanding the purpose and usage of specific M language components.

IntelliSense:

IntelliSense is a powerful feature in Power Query that enhances code development by providing context-aware suggestions and insights as users write M formulas.

1. Function and Column Names:

- When typing a function or column name, IntelliSense offers a dropdown menu of suggestions, drawing from the available dataset. This assists users in selecting the correct names and reduces the likelihood of typographical errors.

2. Parameter Information:

- While entering parameters for functions, IntelliSense provides information about the expected data types and order of parameters. This helps users input accurate and well-structured function arguments.

3. Table and Column References:

- IntelliSense also facilitates referencing tables and columns by offering a list of available options. This ensures precision in referring to specific elements within the dataset.

Tips for Efficient Use:

1. Keyboard Shortcuts:

- Learn and utilize keyboard shortcuts for common actions in the Formula Bar. For instance, pressing "Ctrl + E" in the Formula Bar expands the editor to a full-screen view, providing a more spacious coding environment.

2. Error Highlighting:

- Pay attention to error highlighting in the Formula Bar. Incorrect syntax or unresolved references are often flagged, allowing users to address issues promptly.

3. Experiment with IntelliSense:

- Experiment with IntelliSense suggestions to explore available functions and columns. This exploration can enhance users' familiarity with the dataset and M language capabilities.

Conclusion:

Mastering the Formula Bar and IntelliSense in Power Query empowers users to write, edit, and debug M formulas efficiently. These tools not only facilitate accurate coding but also contribute to a more intuitive and user-friendly experience within the Power Query Editor. As we proceed in this guide, incorporating these techniques will prove instrumental in harnessing the full potential of the M language for business intelligence tasks.

7. Business Intelligence Concepts

7.1. Key Performance Indicators (KPIs) and metrics

In the realm of Business Intelligence (BI), understanding and effectively leveraging Key Performance Indicators (KPIs) and metrics is essential for informed decision-making and performance assessment. This section explores the fundamental concepts of KPIs and metrics, elucidating their significance in the business intelligence landscape.

Key Performance Indicators (KPIs):

1. Definition:

 - KPIs are quantifiable measures used to evaluate the performance of an organization, department, or individual against strategic goals. They serve as benchmarks for assessing progress and aligning efforts with overarching objectives.

2. Characteristics of Effective KPIs:

 - *Relevance:* KPIs should directly align with business objectives and provide meaningful insights.

 - *Measurability:* KPIs must be quantifiable, allowing for objective assessment.

 - *Timeliness:* KPIs should provide real-time or timely information for responsive decision-making.

 - *Consistency:* KPIs should be consistently measured over time to track trends and performance changes.

3. Examples of KPIs:

 - *Revenue Growth Rate:* Measures the percentage increase in revenue over a specific period.

- *Customer Satisfaction Index:* Gauges the satisfaction levels of customers through surveys or feedback.

- *Employee Productivity:* Tracks the efficiency of employees in achieving predefined tasks.

Metrics:

1. Definition:

- Metrics are specific, measurable values that quantify different aspects of business performance. They are the building blocks that contribute to the calculation and assessment of KPIs.

2. Relationship Between Metrics and KPIs:

- Metrics are the individual data points or variables used to calculate KPIs. While a metric might represent a standalone value, a KPI often comprises multiple related metrics to provide a comprehensive performance indicator.

3. Categories of Metrics:

- *Financial Metrics:* Relate to monetary aspects, such as revenue, profit margin, and return on investment.

- *Operational Metrics:* Focus on the efficiency of internal processes, inventory management, and resource utilization.

- *Customer Metrics:* Reflect customer-related data, including acquisition cost, retention rate, and customer lifetime value.

4. Selecting Appropriate Metrics:

- The choice of metrics depends on the specific goals and objectives of the organization. Metrics should align with the strategic focus and be capable of influencing decision-making.

5. Using Power Query for KPIs and Metrics:

- Power Query facilitates the extraction, transformation, and loading (ETL) of data, enabling the creation of calculated columns and measures that contribute to the calculation of KPIs and metrics. By leveraging Power Query's capabilities, users can integrate data from various sources to derive meaningful performance indicators.

Understanding the interplay between KPIs and metrics is fundamental for establishing a robust business intelligence framework. In subsequent sections, we will explore data visualization techniques and common BI tools to effectively communicate and derive insights from these performance indicators.

7.2. Data visualization and dashboards

In the realm of Business Intelligence (BI), effective data visualization is a cornerstone for conveying insights and facilitating informed decision-making. This section delves into the principles of data visualization and the creation of impactful dashboards using Power Query.

Understanding Data Visualization:

Data visualization involves the graphical representation of data to uncover patterns, trends, and relationships that might be obscured in raw data. It transforms complex datasets into visual formats that are easy to comprehend, enabling stakeholders to derive actionable insights swiftly.

Example Scenario:

Consider a sales team tracking monthly performance metrics. Using Power Query, you can aggregate sales data and create visually engaging charts, such as line graphs or bar charts, to showcase sales trends over time. This visual representation makes it easier for stakeholders to identify peak sales periods, track growth, and pinpoint areas that require attention.

Principles of Effective Dashboards:

Creating an impactful dashboard involves thoughtful design and consideration of the end-users. A well-designed dashboard should be intuitive, informative, and capable of providing a holistic view of key performance indicators (KPIs).

Example Scenario:

Imagine designing a financial dashboard for a company's executives. Utilizing Power Query, you can connect to relevant financial data sources, aggregate key financial metrics, and present them through visually appealing gauges or scorecards. This dashboard can include KPIs like revenue, expenses, and profit margins, providing a real-time snapshot of the company's financial health.

Power Query for Data Preparation:

Power Query plays a pivotal role in data preparation for effective visualization. It allows users to clean, transform, and shape data before it is used in visualization tools like Power BI. This ensures that the data is accurate, consistent, and ready for insightful visualization.

Example Scenario:

Suppose you have sales data with irregularities or missing values. Through Power Query, you can apply data cleaning transformations to handle missing data, remove duplicates, and standardize formats. The cleaned dataset can then be seamlessly integrated into Power BI for visualization, ensuring the accuracy of the visual insights presented.

Interactive Dashboards for Exploration:

Power Query facilitates the creation of interactive dashboards that empower users to explore data dynamically. Features like slicers, filters, and drill-down options enhance the user experience, allowing stakeholders to delve deeper into specific aspects of the data.

Example Scenario:

Imagine building a regional sales dashboard with Power Query. Users can interactively explore sales performance by selecting specific regions, time periods, or product categories. Power Query enables the dynamic updating of visuals based on user selections, providing a personalized and interactive exploration experience.

This section aims to equip readers with the knowledge and skills needed to leverage Power Query for effective data visualization and dashboard creation in the context of Business Intelligence. Through practical examples and hands-on guidance, users can elevate their ability to transform raw data into compelling visual narratives that drive meaningful business decisions.

7.3. Common BI tools and techniques

In the realm of Business Intelligence (BI), various tools and techniques empower organizations to extract actionable insights from their data. This section explores commonly used BI tools and techniques, shedding light on their functionalities and contributions to the BI landscape.

Common BI Tools:

1. Microsoft Power BI:

- *Overview:* Power BI is a versatile and user-friendly BI tool developed by Microsoft. It facilitates data visualization, business analytics, and the creation of interactive reports and dashboards.

- *Key Features:*

  - Seamless integration with various data sources.

  - Intuitive drag-and-drop interface for report creation.

  - Robust sharing and collaboration features.

2. Tableau:

- *Overview:* Tableau is a widely adopted BI and data visualization tool known for its powerful analytics capabilities. It enables users to create visually compelling dashboards and reports.

- *Key Features:*

  - Rich data visualization options.

  - Strong support for real-time data analysis.

  - Interactive dashboards for dynamic exploration.

3. QlikView/Qlik Sense:

- *Overview:* QlikView and Qlik Sense are BI tools that use associative data modeling to provide a comprehensive view of data relationships. They emphasize user-driven exploration of data.

- *Key Features:*

  - Associative data model for intuitive exploration.

  - Drag-and-drop interface for rapid report creation.

  - Collaborative analytics capabilities.

4. Google Data Studio:

- *Overview:* Google Data Studio is a free, cloud-based BI tool that integrates seamlessly with other Google products. It allows users to create dynamic and interactive reports.

- *Key Features:*

  - Direct connections to various data sources.

  - Customizable and shareable reports.

  - Collaboration features for real-time editing.

Common BI Techniques:

1. Data Visualization:

- *Definition:* Data visualization involves representing data in graphical or visual formats, making it easier to comprehend trends, patterns, and insights.

- *Techniques:*

  - Charts and graphs (bar charts, line charts, pie charts).

  - Heatmaps and treemaps.

  - Geographic maps for spatial analysis.

2. Dashboards:

- *Definition:* Dashboards are interactive and consolidated displays of key metrics and visualizations, providing a holistic view of business performance.

- *Techniques:*

  - KPI cards for key metrics.

  - Drill-down capabilities for detailed analysis.

  - Integration of multiple visualizations for a comprehensive overview.

3. Predictive Analytics:

- *Definition:* Predictive analytics involves using statistical algorithms and machine learning techniques to identify future trends or outcomes based on historical data.

- *Techniques:*

  - Regression analysis for trend prediction.

  - Classification algorithms for categorization.

  - Time series analysis for forecasting.

4. Data Mining:

- *Definition:* Data mining is the process of discovering patterns and relationships in large datasets.

- Techniques:

  - Association rule mining for discovering correlations.

  - Clustering for grouping similar data points.

  - Decision trees for classification.

By understanding and leveraging these common BI tools and techniques, organizations can enhance their analytical capabilities, transforming raw data into actionable insights for strategic decision-making. The integration of these tools and techniques, combined with a solid foundation in KPIs, metrics, and data visualization, forms the bedrock of a robust Business Intelligence strategy.

PART 2
Power Query in Practice

8. Data Analysis with Power Query

8.1. Exploring and analyzing data using Power Query

In the dynamic landscape of data analysis, Power Query emerges as a powerful tool within the Microsoft Power BI ecosystem. This section explores the fundamental aspects of exploring and analyzing data using Power Query, shedding light on its capabilities for efficient data transformation and insightful analysis.

Understanding Power Query:

1. Data Exploration:

   - Power Query serves as a robust data exploration tool, allowing users to connect to various data sources, preview data, and gain a preliminary understanding of the dataset's structure and content.

2. Source Connectivity:

   - Power Query facilitates seamless connectivity to diverse data sources, including databases, spreadsheets, online services, and more. Users can import data directly or establish dynamic connections for live updates.

3. Data Profiling:

- Utilizing Power Query's data profiling features, users can quickly assess the quality and characteristics of the data. This includes identifying data types, checking for missing values, and understanding distribution patterns.

Data Transformation and Analysis:

1. Column Operations:

- Power Query allows users to perform a myriad of operations on columns, including renaming, duplicating, and changing data types. Additionally, users can create custom columns based on calculations or conditional logic.

```
// Example: Creating a new column 'TotalSales' by summing 'Sales' and 'Discount'

#"Added Custom" = Table.AddColumn(Source, "TotalSales", each [Sales] + [Discount])
```

2. Data Filtering and Sorting:

- Power Query enables the application of filters to selectively retrieve and manipulate data based on specified criteria. Sorting options allow users to arrange data in ascending or descending order.

```
// Example: Filtering rows where 'Category' is 'Electronics'

#"Filtered Rows" = Table.SelectRows(Source, each [Category] = "Electronics")
```

3. Aggregations and Grouping:

- Power Query supports aggregations and grouping operations, allowing users to summarize data based on specific criteria. This is particularly useful for creating summary tables or obtaining key insights.

```
// Example: Grouping data by 'Year' and calculating the total sales for each year
```

```
#"Grouped Rows" = Table.Group(Source, "Year", {{"Total Sales", each List.Sum([Sales]),
type number}})
```

Visualization and Iterative Analysis:

1. Previewing Data Changes:

- Power Query offers a real-time preview of data changes during the transformation process. Users can iteratively adjust and refine their transformations, immediately observing the impact on the dataset.

2. Data Profiling Visualizations:

- Visualizations within Power Query, such as histograms and distribution charts, provide visual insights into the characteristics of the data. This aids in identifying patterns, outliers, and potential areas for further exploration.

```
// Example: Creating a histogram for the 'Sales' column

#"Sales Histogram" = Table.Histogram(Source, {"Sales"})
```

3. Query Dependencies:

- Power Query displays the dependency chain of applied transformations, offering a clear understanding of the sequence of operations. This transparency aids in troubleshooting and maintaining a structured and organized query.

By leveraging the capabilities of Power Query for data exploration and analysis, users can transform raw data into meaningful insights, setting the stage for comprehensive business intelligence and decision-making within the Power BI environment.

Example Scenario: Exploring and Analyzing Sales Data

Suppose we have a dataset containing sales information for a retail business, and we want to explore and analyze the data using Power Query.

1. Data Exploration:

- Open Power BI Desktop and go to the Power Query Editor.

- Connect to the dataset (e.g., a CSV file or a database table).

- In the Power Query Editor, explore the data using the "Data Preview" and "Data Profiling" features to understand the structure and characteristics of the dataset.

2. Data Transformation:

- Create a calculated column to represent the total sales for each transaction:

```
// Adding a calculated column 'TotalSales' by summing 'Quantity' and 'Price'
#"Added Custom" = Table.AddColumn(Source, "TotalSales", each [Quantity] [Price])
```

- Apply a filter to focus on sales data within a specific time frame:

```
// Filtering rows for sales in the year 2022
#"Filtered Rows" = Table.SelectRows(#"Added Custom", each Date.Year([Date]) = 2022)
```

- Group the data by product category and calculate the total sales for each category:

// Grouping data by 'Category' and calculating total sales

#"Grouped Rows" = Table.Group(#"Filtered Rows", "Category", {{"Total Sales", each List.Sum([TotalSales]), type number}})

3. Visualization and Iterative Analysis:

- Create a histogram to visualize the distribution of total sales within each product category:

// Creating a histogram for 'Total Sales' within each category

#"Sales Histogram" = Table.Histogram(#"Grouped Rows", {"Total Sales"})

- Use the preview feature to observe the impact of different transformations on the dataset in real-time. For instance, try adjusting the date filter or modifying the calculated column to observe immediate changes.

4. Query Dependencies:

- Navigate to the "View" tab in Power Query Editor and select "Query Dependencies" to visualize the applied transformations and their dependencies. This helps in understanding the sequence of operations.

This example showcases how Power Query can be used to explore and analyze sales data iteratively. By leveraging data transformations, filtering, grouping, and visualization techniques, users can gain valuable insights into their dataset, paving the way for more advanced business intelligence tasks within the Power BI environment.

8.2. Creating calculated columns and measures

In the realm of data analysis using Power Query, the ability to create calculated columns and measures is a crucial skill. This section delves into the concepts and techniques involved in generating calculated columns and measures, showcasing how these elements contribute to enhanced data analysis within the Power BI ecosystem.

Understanding Calculated Columns:

1. Definition:

 - Calculated columns are custom columns created within Power Query that derive their values through specified calculations or expressions. They allow users to introduce new data elements based on existing columns.

2. Creation Process:

 - Calculated columns are typically created using the "Add Column" tab in Power Query. Users can define the calculation logic using the M language or Power Query's formula language.

```
// Example: Creating a calculated column 'TotalRevenue' by multiplying 'Price' and 'Quantity'
#"Added Custom" = Table.AddColumn(Source, "TotalRevenue", each [Price] [Quantity])
```

3. Use Cases:

 - Calculated columns are beneficial for introducing new dimensions or metrics into the dataset, such as calculating total revenue, profit margins, or customer segment classifications.

Leveraging Measures for Aggregation:

1. Definition:

- Measures are dynamic aggregations or calculations applied to the entire dataset or specific subsets. Unlike calculated columns, measures are created within the Power BI report and can utilize Data Analysis Expressions (DAX), a formula language.

2. Creation Process:

- Measures are generated in the "Modeling" tab of Power BI Desktop. Users define DAX expressions to perform aggregations, calculations, or logic that dynamically adjusts based on context.

```
// Example: Creating a measure 'AverageSales' to calculate the average of 'Sales' column

AverageSales = AVERAGE('Sales')
```

3. Use Cases:

- Measures are powerful for dynamic calculations in reports and dashboards, such as calculating averages, totals, or percentages. They respond dynamically to slicers, filters, and changes in data context.

Differentiating Between Calculated Columns and Measures:

1. Static vs. Dynamic:

- Calculated columns are static and part of the dataset, while measures are dynamic and respond to user interactions within reports.

2. Resource Impact:

- Calculated columns consume more memory as they are part of the dataset, while measures are evaluated on the fly, minimizing resource consumption.

Best Practices and Tips:

1. Efficiency Considerations:

- Use calculated columns judiciously to avoid unnecessary data bloat. Reserve them for calculations that genuinely require a new column in the dataset.

2. DAX Proficiency:

- Enhance DAX proficiency for creating sophisticated measures. DAX offers a wide range of functions for complex calculations.

3. Context Awareness:

- Understand the importance of context in DAX expressions for measures. Context plays a crucial role in determining how measures respond to different user interactions.

By mastering the creation of calculated columns and measures, users can elevate their data analysis capabilities within Power Query and Power BI. These elements form the building blocks for deriving meaningful insights and actionable intelligence from raw datasets.

Let's walk through an example of creating calculated columns and measures using Power Query and Power BI. For this illustration, let's consider a sales dataset with information about products, quantities sold, prices, and dates.

Example: Sales Dataset Analysis

1. Calculated Column: Total Revenue

In this scenario, we want to create a calculated column named 'TotalRevenue' by multiplying the 'Price' and 'Quantity' columns.

Power Query Steps:

1. Open Power BI Desktop and load your sales dataset.

2. Go to the "Home" tab and click on "Transform Data" to open the Power Query Editor.

3. In the Power Query Editor, go to the "Add Column" tab.

4. Click on "Custom Column" and enter the following formula:

```
// Creating a calculated column 'TotalRevenue' by multiplying 'Price' and 'Quantity'
TotalRevenue = [Price]  [Quantity]
```

5. Click "OK" to create the new column.

6. Close and apply the changes, and the 'TotalRevenue' column will be added to your dataset.

2. Measure: Average Sales

Now, let's create a measure named 'AverageSales' to calculate the average of the 'Sales' column.

Power BI Steps:

1. Go to the "Modeling" tab in Power BI Desktop.

2. Click on "New Measure" in the ribbon.

3. Enter the following DAX formula for the average sales:

```
// Creating a measure 'AverageSales' to calculate the average of 'Sales' column
AverageSales = AVERAGE('Sales')
```

4. Press Enter to create the measure.

5. You can now use the 'AverageSales' measure in your reports and visuals.

3. Using Calculated Column and Measure in a Report:

1. Create a new report page in Power BI Desktop.

2. Drag the 'TotalRevenue' calculated column into a table or matrix visual to display total revenue for each transaction.

3. Place the 'AverageSales' measure in a card visual to show the average sales across the entire dataset.

4. You can add filters, slicers, or other visuals to interactively analyze the data. For example, you can add a slicer for the 'Year' column to see average sales for a specific year.

Best Practices:

- Use calculated columns for static, row-level calculations that you want to store in your dataset permanently.

- Use measures for dynamic, context-aware aggregations that respond to changes in filters, slicers, or other user interactions.

- Be mindful of the impact on performance, especially when dealing with large datasets. Avoid unnecessary calculated columns that might lead to data bloat.

This example demonstrates the practical application of creating calculated columns and measures in Power Query and Power BI for effective data analysis and reporting.

8.3. Filtering and slicers for interactive analysis

In the realm of data analysis using Power Query, the ability to apply filters and utilize slicers is pivotal for creating interactive and dynamic reports. This section delves into the concepts and techniques involved in leveraging filtering and slicers to facilitate an immersive analysis experience within Power BI.

Understanding Filtering in Power Query:

1. Filtering Rows:

   - Filtering is a fundamental operation in Power Query that allows users to selectively include or exclude rows based on specified conditions. This ensures that only relevant data is included in the analysis.

```
// Example: Filtering rows for sales in the year 2022
#"Filtered Rows" = Table.SelectRows(Source, each Date.Year([Date]) = 2022)
```

2. Filtering Columns:

- Power Query enables users to filter columns to include only the necessary data fields in the analysis. This can improve performance and streamline the dataset for a more focused examination.

```
// Example: Keeping only 'ProductID' and 'Sales' columns
#"Kept Columns" = Table.SelectColumns(Source, {"ProductID", "Sales"})
```

3. Advanced Filtering:

- Advanced filtering options, such as custom filtering logic or filtering based on multiple conditions, provide users with fine-grained control over data inclusion.

```
// Example: Filtering rows where both 'Quantity' and 'Price' are greater than 10
#"Filtered Rows" = Table.SelectRows(Source, each [Quantity] > 10 and [Price] > 10)
```

Utilizing Slicers in Power BI Reports:

1. Definition of Slicers:

- Slicers are visual controls within Power BI reports that allow users to filter data interactively. They provide an intuitive way to dynamically adjust the data displayed in visuals.

2. Creating Slicers:

- To create a slicer, select a field (e.g., 'Year') in the Fields pane, right-click, and choose "Add as Slicer." This creates a visual slicer that users can interact with.

3. Applying Slicer Filters:

- Users can use slicers to filter data in visuals, such as tables or charts, by clicking on specific values. Slicer filters dynamically adjust the data displayed based on the user's selection.

4. Multi-Select and Cross-Filtering:

- Slicers support multi-select options, enabling users to choose multiple values simultaneously. Additionally, slicers can implement cross-filtering, influencing other visuals on the report page.

Dynamic Analysis with Filtering and Slicers:

1. Interactive Dashboards:

- By combining filters, slicers, and visuals, users can create interactive dashboards that respond dynamically to user interactions. This enhances the user experience and allows for on-the-fly analysis.

2. Dynamic Drill-Downs:

- Slicers can be utilized to create drill-down functionalities, enabling users to delve into specific subsets of data and explore details at various levels of granularity.

Best Practices and Tips:

1. Optimize Slicer Layout:

- Arrange slicers in a user-friendly layout to enhance the overall look and feel of the report. Use the formatting options to customize the appearance.

2. Understand Cross-Filtering Behavior:

- Be aware of how cross-filtering behaves in different scenarios. Understanding the relationships between tables in the dataset is crucial for accurate cross-filtering.

3. Utilize Slicer Styles:

- Power BI provides built-in slicer styles or allows customization. Choose styles that align with the report's aesthetics and ensure clarity in user interaction.

By mastering filtering techniques and leveraging slicers effectively, users can create engaging and dynamic Power BI reports that empower end-users to explore data interactively and derive meaningful insights during the analysis process.

Example Scenario: Sales Analysis with Filtering and Slicers

1. Filtering in Power Query:

Suppose we have a sales dataset and want to analyze data for the year 2022 and for products where both the quantity and price are greater than 10.

Power Query Steps:

1. Open Power BI Desktop and load your sales dataset.

2. Go to the "Home" tab and click on "Transform Data" to open the Power Query Editor.

3. To filter rows for the year 2022:

```
// Filtering rows for sales in the year 2022
```

```
#"Filtered Rows" = Table.SelectRows(Source, each Date.Year([Date]) = 2022)
```

4. To filter rows where both quantity and price are greater than 10:

```
// Filtering rows where both 'Quantity' and 'Price' are greater than 10
#"Filtered Rows" = Table.SelectRows(Source, each [Quantity] > 10 and [Price] > 10)
```

5. Close and apply the changes, and your dataset is now filtered based on the specified conditions.

2. Creating Slicers in Power BI:

Now, let's create slicers for the 'Year' and 'Product Category' fields to allow interactive analysis.

Power BI Steps:

1. In Power BI Desktop, go to the "View" tab and select "Slicer" to add a slicer visual to your report.

2. In the Fields pane, drag the 'Year' field into the slicer visual. This creates a slicer control.

3. Repeat the process to add another slicer for the 'Product Category' field.

4. Arrange the slicers on your report canvas for a clean layout.

3. Applying Slicer Filters:

1. Click on a specific year in the 'Year' slicer. You'll notice that all visuals on the report page are dynamically filtered to show data only for the selected year.

2. Similarly, use the 'Product Category' slicer to filter data for a specific product category.

3. Experiment with multi-select options in slicers to analyze data for multiple years or product categories simultaneously.

4. Dynamic Analysis:

1. Create visuals like tables, charts, or graphs on the report page that respond to slicer interactions.

2. For instance, create a bar chart showing total sales by product category. As you interact with slicers, the chart dynamically adjusts to display sales data based on your selections.

Best Practices:

1. Optimize Slicer Layout:

 - Arrange slicers in a logical and user-friendly layout on the report canvas. Utilize formatting options to enhance the visual appeal.

2. Understand Cross-Filtering Behavior:

 - Be aware of how slicer interactions might cross-filter other visuals. Verify relationships between tables for accurate cross-filtering.

3. Dynamic Drill-Downs:

- Use slicers to create drill-down experiences. For instance, clicking on a specific product category might reveal details about individual products.

By following these steps and best practices, you can create an interactive sales analysis report in Power BI, allowing users to dynamically explore and analyze data using filtering and slicers.

9. Creating Reports and Dashboards

9.1. Using Power BI Desktop to create reports

Power BI Desktop serves as a robust tool for crafting insightful reports that transform raw data into meaningful visualizations. This section provides a step-by-step guide on leveraging Power BI Desktop to create compelling reports, ensuring that data-driven insights are effectively communicated.

Getting Started:

1. Launching Power BI Desktop:

  - Open Power BI Desktop on your machine, and you'll be greeted with a welcoming interface.

2. Connecting to Data:

  - Click on the "Get Data" option to connect to your data source. Power BI supports various sources such as Excel, databases, online services, and more.

3. Importing and Transforming Data:

  - Import the data into Power BI Desktop and utilize the Power Query Editor to shape and transform the data as needed. This step ensures that the dataset is refined for report creation.

Building the Report:

1. Data Visualization Basics:

  - Drag and drop fields from your dataset onto the report canvas. Power BI will automatically suggest visualizations based on the data types.

2. Choosing Visualizations:

- Explore the wide array of visualizations available in the Visualizations pane. Select the appropriate chart or graph based on the nature of your data and the story you want to convey.

3. Customizing Visuals:

- Customize each visual by adjusting formatting options, colors, and titles. Power BI Desktop offers extensive customization features to enhance the aesthetics of your report.

```
// Example: Changing the color of a bar chart

Bar Chart Color = SELECTEDVALUE('Sales'[Product]) = "Product A" ? "#3498db" : "#e74c3c"
```

4. Page Layout and Organization:

- Utilize the Pages pane to create multiple pages for different aspects of your report. Arrange visuals on each page to provide a structured and logical flow.

Interactivity and Drill-Downs:

1. Slicers and Filters:

- Incorporate slicers for interactive filtering. Slicers allow end-users to dynamically adjust data on the report, providing a more engaging experience.

2. Drill-Down Functionality:

- Implement drill-downs by creating hierarchies in your visuals. For example, allow users to drill down from a yearly overview to monthly or daily details.

Optimizing Report Performance:

1. Data Model Optimization:

- Ensure that your data model is optimized for performance. Remove unnecessary columns, create relationships between tables, and manage data types efficiently.

2. Data Refresh Settings:

- Set up scheduled data refresh to keep your reports up-to-date with the latest data from the source. This is crucial for maintaining the accuracy of insights.

Previewing and Testing:

1. Report Preview:

- Use the "View" tab to preview your report and test interactivity. Ensure that visuals respond appropriately to filters, slicers, and other user interactions.

2. Troubleshooting:

- If issues arise, leverage the "Troubleshoot" features to identify and resolve errors in your report. Power BI Desktop provides helpful diagnostic tools.

Saving and Publishing:

1. Saving the Report:

- Save your Power BI Desktop file (.pbix) to ensure that your work is preserved. Regularly save iterations as you make progress.

2. Publishing to Power BI Service:

- Click on "Publish" to upload your report to the Power BI service. This enables sharing and collaboration with stakeholders.

By following these steps, users can harness the full potential of Power BI Desktop to create visually compelling and informative reports. The next sections will delve into designing visually appealing reports and sharing insights with stakeholders, complementing the report creation process.

9.2. Designing visually appealing and informative reports

Creating visually appealing reports is paramount for effectively communicating data-driven insights to stakeholders. This section outlines key principles and techniques for designing engaging and informative reports using Power BI Desktop.

Principles of Report Design:

1. Clarity and Simplicity:

- Prioritize clarity by presenting information in a straightforward manner. Avoid unnecessary complexity and focus on delivering a clear narrative.

2. Consistency:

- Maintain consistency in visual elements, such as colors, fonts, and formatting. Consistency enhances the professional look of the report and improves user experience.

3. Hierarchy and Flow:

- Establish a logical hierarchy and flow in your report. Arrange visuals in a sequence that guides users through the story you want to convey, leading from key insights to supporting details.

4. Whitespace and Layout:

- Utilize whitespace effectively to reduce visual clutter. Ensure a balanced layout that enhances readability and draws attention to essential elements.

Effective Visualizations:

1. Appropriate Chart Selection:

- Choose the right chart type for the data you're presenting. Bar charts, line charts, and pie charts serve different purposes, so align your choice with the nature of your data.

2. Color Usage:

- Employ a consistent color palette that aligns with your organization's branding. Use color strategically to highlight key points, but avoid excessive use that may distract from the data.

```
// Example: Using conditional formatting to highlight positive and negative values

Positive-Negative Color = IF([Revenue] > 0, "#2ecc71", "#e74c3c")
```

3. Annotations and Labels:

- Add relevant annotations and labels to provide context and clarify data points. Annotations help stakeholders interpret visuals accurately.

4. Conditional Formatting:

- Apply conditional formatting to highlight specific ranges or trends in your data. For instance, color-coding cells in a table based on certain criteria enhances visibility.

// Example: Conditional formatting for a heatmap

Heatmap Color = Color.FromRgb(255, 0, 0) // Red for high values

Interactive Elements:

1. Slicers and Filters:

- Incorporate slicers and filters for user interactivity. Allow stakeholders to explore data dynamically, making the report more engaging and tailored to individual needs.

2. Drill-Downs and Hierarchies:

- Implement drill-down features and hierarchies in visuals. This enables users to delve deeper into specific aspects of the data, enhancing the granularity of analysis.

Layout and Composition:

1. Dashboard Composition:

- When designing dashboards, consider how visuals are arranged. Dashboards should provide a holistic view of the data, offering a quick overview before stakeholders delve into specific reports.

2. KPIs and Key Metrics:

- Highlight key performance indicators (KPIs) prominently. Use cards, gauges, or other visuals to showcase critical metrics that align with business objectives.

Iterative Design Process:

1. Get Feedback:

- Seek feedback from stakeholders during the design process. Iteratively refine the report based on input to ensure it meets their expectations.

2. Usability Testing:

- Conduct usability testing to evaluate how well stakeholders can navigate and understand the report. Adjust elements that may cause confusion or hinder usability.

Best Practices:

1. Accessibility:

- Ensure that your report is accessible to a diverse audience. Consider color-blindness and other accessibility standards in your design.

2. Storytelling:

- Weave a narrative through your report. Guide stakeholders through the data, explaining key findings and their implications.

By adhering to these design principles and incorporating effective visualizations, interactive elements, and thoughtful layout, you can create visually appealing and informative reports that resonate with stakeholders and facilitate data-driven decision-making.

9.3. Sharing reports and insights with stakeholders

Once you've crafted insightful reports in Power BI Desktop, the next crucial step is to share these reports and the derived insights with stakeholders. This section provides guidance on the various methods and best practices for sharing your Power BI reports effectively.

Power BI Service:

1. Publishing to Power BI Service:

- After creating a report in Power BI Desktop, use the "Publish" feature to upload your report (.pbix file) to the Power BI service. This cloud-based platform facilitates collaboration and sharing.

2. Power BI Workspace:

- Organize your reports in workspaces within the Power BI service. Workspaces serve as collaborative environments where stakeholders can access and interact with shared reports.

Sharing Options:

1. Share a Dashboard:

- Create dashboards within the Power BI service to aggregate key visuals from multiple reports. Share these dashboards with stakeholders to provide a consolidated view of critical metrics.

2. Sharing a Report:

- Share individual reports directly from the Power BI service. Stakeholders with the appropriate permissions can view and interact with the report, exploring data and gaining insights.

Collaboration Features:

1. Commenting and Annotations:

- Encourage collaboration by enabling commenting on specific visuals within reports. Stakeholders can provide feedback, ask questions, or share additional insights directly within the report.

2. Sharing with External Users:

- Extend collaboration beyond your organization by sharing reports or dashboards with external users. Power BI allows secure sharing with stakeholders outside your organization, ensuring data privacy.

Power BI Apps:

1. Creating Apps:

- Package your reports, dashboards, and datasets into Power BI apps. Apps provide a streamlined way to share a collection of related content with stakeholders, simplifying access.

2. Distributing Apps:

- Distribute your Power BI app to specific users or make it available publicly in the Power BI AppSource. Apps are an efficient way to deliver a curated analytics experience.

Scheduled Email Subscriptions:

1. Subscription Setup:

- Configure scheduled email subscriptions to send specific report visuals or dashboards to stakeholders at predefined intervals. This ensures that stakeholders receive regular updates without actively accessing the Power BI service.

2. Personalized Subscriptions:

- Tailor subscriptions based on individual stakeholder preferences. Allow users to choose the frequency and content they wish to receive, fostering a personalized experience.

Embedding Reports:

1. Embedding in Websites or Applications:

   - Embed Power BI reports or visuals directly into websites or custom applications. This enables stakeholders to access insights seamlessly within familiar environments.

2. Controlled Access:

   - Implement row-level security and authentication to control access when embedding reports. Ensure that stakeholders only see the data relevant to their roles or permissions.

Best Practices:

1. Data Refresh Schedules:

   - Set up regular data refresh schedules to keep shared reports updated with the latest data. This is crucial for maintaining the accuracy of insights over time.

2. Training and Documentation:

   - Provide training materials and documentation for stakeholders to navigate and interpret reports effectively. This enhances user adoption and ensures stakeholders can derive maximum value.

3. Security Considerations:

   - Understand and implement Power BI's security features. Define roles, manage permissions, and apply row-level security to safeguard sensitive data.

Sharing reports and insights with stakeholders is a collaborative process that involves choosing the right sharing methods, ensuring data security, and facilitating an accessible and insightful analytics experience. By employing these best practices, you can effectively communicate data-driven insights and empower stakeholders to make informed decisions.

10. Sharing and Collaborating

10.1. Publishing reports to Power BI Service

In this section, we'll explore the process of publishing reports from Power BI Desktop to the Power BI Service. Publishing is a crucial step that allows you to share your reports with stakeholders, enabling collaboration and access to real-time data.

Steps to Publish a Report:

1. Save Your Power BI Desktop File:

- Before publishing, ensure that you've saved your Power BI Desktop (.pbix) file. This file contains the report layout, visuals, and connections to the underlying data.

2. Sign in to Power BI Account:

- Open Power BI Desktop and sign in with your Power BI account. If you don't have an account, you'll need to create one.

3. Click on "Publish":

- In Power BI Desktop, navigate to the "Home" tab, and click on the "Publish" button. This action initiates the process of uploading your report to the Power BI Service.

4. Select a Workspace:

- Choose the workspace in the Power BI Service where you want to publish your report. Workspaces serve as collaborative environments, and you can organize content based on projects, teams, or departments.

5. Review the Upload:

- Power BI Desktop will display a progress bar indicating the upload status. Once completed, a confirmation message will notify you that the report has been successfully published to the selected workspace.

Key Considerations:

1. Data Source Connectivity:

- Ensure that the data sources used in your Power BI Desktop file are accessible in the Power BI Service. This may involve setting up data source credentials for secure connections.

2. Dataset Refresh:

- Configure dataset refresh settings in the Power BI Service if your report relies on scheduled updates. This ensures that the data in the Power BI Service remains current.

Collaboration in Power BI Service:

1. Accessing the Published Report:

- Stakeholders with appropriate permissions can access the published report by logging into the Power BI Service. They can explore the report, interact with visuals, and gain insights.

2. Sharing and Permissions:

- Manage sharing and permissions for the report within the Power BI Service. Define who can view, edit, or build upon the report to control access.

Version History:

1. Viewing Version History:

- Explore version history in the Power BI Service to track changes made to the report over time. This feature aids in understanding modifications and reverting to previous versions if needed.

2. Collaborative Editing:

- Collaborate with team members by allowing simultaneous editing of the report. This facilitates real-time collaboration and updates within the Power BI Service.

Best Practices:

1. Organize Content in Workspaces:

- Use workspaces to organize content logically. Create workspaces for specific projects, teams, or departments to streamline collaboration.

2. Communicate Changes:

- Communicate changes to stakeholders when publishing updates to reports. Providing context about modifications enhances the understanding of the evolving data story.

3. Utilize Comments and Annotations:

- Encourage stakeholders to use comments and annotations within the Power BI Service to provide feedback or ask questions. This fosters collaboration and a shared understanding of the data.

By following these steps and best practices, you can seamlessly publish your Power BI reports to the Power BI Service, opening the door to collaborative data analysis and insights sharing with stakeholders.

10.2. Collaborating with others on reports and data models

Collaboration is a key aspect of Power BI, enabling teams to work together efficiently on reports and data models. This section delves into effective strategies for collaborative work in Power BI, ensuring seamless teamwork and shared insights.

Collaborative Editing:

1. Simultaneous Editing in Power BI Service:

- Power BI Service allows multiple users to collaborate on a report simultaneously. This means that team members can make edits or additions in real-time, fostering a collaborative environment.

2. Visibility of Changes:

- Users collaborating on a report can see each other's changes instantly. This feature promotes transparency and ensures that team members are aware of modifications made by their colleagues.

Version Control:

1. Tracking Changes with Version History:

- Power BI Service maintains a version history that records changes made to the report. Users can review this history, compare versions, and revert to previous states if necessary.

2. Annotation of Versions:

- Annotate significant changes in the version history to provide context to collaborators. This practice aids in understanding the evolution of the report and the rationale behind specific modifications.

Collaborative Workspace:

1. Shared Workspaces:

- Utilize shared workspaces for collaborative projects. Workspaces in Power BI Service allow teams to organize content collectively, ensuring a centralized location for collaborative efforts.

2. Access Control in Workspaces:

- Manage access controls within workspaces. Define roles for team members, specifying who can view, edit, or share reports. This ensures that permissions align with team roles and responsibilities.

Communication and Feedback:

1. Commenting on Reports:

- Leverage the commenting feature within Power BI Service to facilitate communication. Users can leave comments on specific visuals or datasets, providing feedback or asking questions.

2. Feedback Loop:

- Encourage an open feedback loop among team members. Regularly solicit input on report design, data models, and insights. Constructive feedback contributes to the refinement of reports.

Data Model Collaboration:

1. Shared Data Models:

- Collaborate on data models by sharing datasets and connections. Power BI Service enables users to work on a shared data model, ensuring consistency and accuracy in data representation.

2. Data Source Connectivity:

- Communicate with team members about data source connectivity. Ensure that everyone has the necessary credentials and access to maintain seamless connections to external data.

Best Practices:

1. Clear Documentation:

- Document data models, transformations, and report logic comprehensively. Clear documentation aids team members in understanding the structure of the data and the report's design.

2. Regular Check-ins:

- Schedule regular check-ins or team meetings to discuss progress, challenges, and goals. This facilitates collaboration and ensures that everyone is aligned with project objectives.

3. Training and Knowledge Sharing:

- Promote training sessions and knowledge-sharing initiatives within the team. Ensuring that all team members are familiar with Power BI features enhances collaborative efforts.

4. Utilize Power BI Apps:

- Package shared reports, dashboards, and data models into Power BI apps for easy distribution within the team or across the organization. Apps simplify the deployment of shared content.

By implementing these collaborative practices, teams can maximize the potential of Power BI, creating a collaborative environment that fosters effective teamwork, enhances report quality, and drives data-driven decision-making across the organization.

10.3. Sharing insights and driving data-driven decisions

In this section, we will explore strategies for sharing insights derived from Power BI reports and how to leverage these insights to drive informed, data-driven decisions within an organization.

Sharing Insights:

1. Creating Shareable Dashboards:

- Build interactive and visually appealing dashboards within Power BI that encapsulate key insights. Dashboards serve as a central hub for stakeholders to access consolidated information.

2. Sharing Dashboards:

- Utilize Power BI Service to share dashboards with stakeholders. Depending on the audience, choose between sharing with specific individuals, groups, or making dashboards public within the organization.

Collaborative Data Exploration:

1. Promoting Data Exploration:

- Encourage stakeholders to explore data independently within shared dashboards. Power BI enables interactive exploration, allowing users to drill down, filter, and analyze data based on their unique perspectives.

2. Embedding Reports:

- Embed reports or visuals into internal websites, portals, or applications. This facilitates seamless access to insights within familiar organizational platforms, promoting widespread data exploration.

Data-Driven Decision-Making:

1. Empowering Stakeholders:

- Empower stakeholders with the skills to interpret and derive insights from Power BI reports. Offer training sessions or workshops to enhance their understanding of the data and the tools available.

2. Aligning Insights with Business Goals:

- Ensure that insights derived from Power BI align with the organization's business goals. Reports and dashboards should focus on relevant key performance indicators (KPIs) and metrics that drive strategic decisions.

Automated Reporting and Alerts:

1. Scheduled Report Distribution:

- Set up automated scheduling for report distribution. Stakeholders can receive regular updates on key metrics, ensuring they stay informed without actively accessing Power BI.

2. Alerts for Anomalies:

- Implement alerting mechanisms for data anomalies. Power BI allows the creation of alerts based on predefined thresholds, notifying stakeholders when metrics deviate from expected values.

Cross-Functional Collaboration:

1. Interdepartmental Collaboration:

- Foster collaboration across departments by sharing relevant reports. Breaking down silos enables teams to collaborate on shared objectives and make decisions based on a holistic view of organizational data.

2. Cross-Functional Insights:

- Develop reports that provide insights cutting across various functional areas. For example, a sales report may integrate data from marketing, enabling a comprehensive understanding of customer engagement.

Measuring Impact:

1. Monitoring Usage and Engagement:

- Track usage metrics within Power BI Service to gauge how stakeholders interact with shared reports. Analyzing user engagement provides insights into the effectiveness of the reports.

2. Feedback Loops:

- Establish feedback loops to collect input from stakeholders. Regularly solicit feedback on report design, usability, and the relevance of insights. This iterative process ensures continuous improvement.

Driving Actionable Decisions:

1. Incorporating Actionable Insights:

- Embed actionable insights within reports. Clearly identify recommendations or actions that stakeholders can take based on the data, facilitating a seamless transition from insights to decision-making.

2. Aligning with Business Processes:

- Integrate Power BI insights into existing business processes. For example, link reports with project management tools or CRM systems to ensure that data-driven decisions align with day-to-day operations.

By focusing on sharing actionable insights and fostering a data-driven decision-making culture, organizations can leverage the full potential of Power BI to drive innovation, optimize processes, and achieve strategic objectives.

11. Data Governance and Security

11.1. Managing access and permissions for data sources

In this section, we delve into the critical aspects of managing access and permissions for data sources within Power BI. Effective management ensures that users have appropriate access to data, aligning with organizational policies and safeguarding sensitive information.

User Roles and Access Control:

1. Defining User Roles:

- Begin by defining distinct user roles based on responsibilities and data requirements. Common roles may include report creators, data analysts, and executives, each requiring different levels of access.

2. Mapping Permissions to Roles:

- Map specific permissions to each user role. Determine who has the authority to view, edit, or manage data sources. Align these permissions with the principle of least privilege to minimize potential risks.

Data Source Connectivity:

1. Credential Management:

- Implement secure credential management for data sources. Avoid hardcoded credentials within Power BI reports and instead utilize service accounts, single sign-on (SSO), or other secure authentication methods.

2. Data Source Encryption:

- Ensure that data transmission between Power BI and external data sources is encrypted. Employ secure connection protocols, such as SSL/TLS, to protect data during transit.

Integration with Identity Providers:

1. Utilizing Single Sign-On (SSO):

- Leverage single sign-on capabilities to streamline user authentication. Integrating Power BI with identity providers ensures a unified and secure authentication process for accessing data sources.

2. Active Directory Integration:

- Integrate Power BI with Active Directory for centralized user management. This allows administrators to control user access, enforce policies, and streamline user provisioning and de-provisioning.

Row-Level Security (RLS):

1. Implementing Row-Level Security:

- Utilize Row-Level Security (RLS) to restrict data access at the row level based on user roles or attributes. This feature ensures that users only see the data relevant to their responsibilities.

2. Role Definition in Power BI Desktop:

- Define roles within Power BI Desktop and associate them with specific filters or rules. When reports are published to the Power BI Service, these roles are enforced to control data visibility.

Audit Logging and Monitoring:

1. Enabling Audit Logging:

- Activate audit logging in Power BI Service to track user activities. Audit logs provide insights into who accessed specific data sources, helping organizations monitor usage and identify potential security issues.

2. Monitoring Usage Metrics:

- Regularly monitor usage metrics within Power BI Service. Analyzing data source access patterns helps identify irregularities, ensuring proactive measures to address any potential security concerns.

Data Source Dependency Mapping:

1. Mapping Data Dependencies:

- Create a comprehensive map of data source dependencies. Understand which reports, dashboards, or datasets rely on specific data sources. This aids in assessing the impact of changes and managing access accordingly.

2. Dependency Documentation:

- Document data source dependencies and their respective access requirements. This documentation serves as a valuable resource for administrators, facilitating efficient management of access permissions.

Regular Security Audits:

1. Conducting Security Audits:

- Periodically conduct security audits to review access permissions, user roles, and data source configurations. This proactive approach helps identify and rectify potential security vulnerabilities.

2. Adapting to Organizational Changes:

- Adjust access permissions in response to organizational changes. As team structures evolve, ensure that access aligns with current roles and responsibilities.

By rigorously managing access and permissions for data sources, organizations can fortify their data governance framework, uphold security standards, and ensure compliance with regulatory requirements. This proactive approach safeguards sensitive information and maintains the integrity of data throughout its lifecycle within the Power BI environment.

11.2. Implementing data governance principles

In this section, we delve into the essential aspects of implementing data governance principles within the Power Query framework. Data governance is a crucial framework that ensures the quality, integrity, and security of data throughout its lifecycle. Here's a comprehensive guide to implementing data governance principles in Power BI.

Data Catalog and Documentation:

1. Building a Data Catalog:

- Establish a centralized data catalog that documents all data sources, including their origins, structures, and relationships. This catalog serves as a comprehensive reference for users and administrators.

2. Metadata Management:

- Implement metadata management practices. Attach relevant metadata, such as data definitions, lineage, and quality assessments, to ensure a clear understanding of the data's context and purpose.

Standardizing Naming Conventions:

1. Consistent Naming Conventions:

- Enforce standardized naming conventions for datasets, reports, and queries. Consistent naming facilitates easy identification and promotes a uniform structure within the Power BI environment.

2. Documentation of Naming Conventions:

- Document and communicate naming conventions to all Power BI users. Clear documentation ensures adherence to standards and minimizes confusion in a collaborative environment.

Data Quality Assurance:

1. Quality Checks in Power Query:

- Integrate data quality checks within Power Query transformations. Implement validation steps to identify and address data anomalies, inconsistencies, or missing values during the data preparation process.

2. Data Profiling:

- Utilize data profiling tools and techniques within Power Query to assess the quality of data. Profiling helps identify patterns, outliers, and potential issues, enabling proactive data cleansing.

Version Control and Change Management:

1. Implementing Version Control:

- Establish version control mechanisms for datasets and reports. This ensures that changes are tracked over time, facilitating rollbacks if needed and providing a historical record of modifications.

2. Change Management Processes:

- Define change management processes for data sources. Clearly outline how changes, updates, or additions to data sources should be documented, tested, and communicated to stakeholders.

Data Ownership and Stewardship:

1. Assigning Data Owners:

- Designate data owners for each dataset or data source. Data owners are responsible for maintaining the accuracy, integrity, and security of the data, fostering a sense of accountability.

2. Data Stewardship Programs:

- Establish data stewardship programs that involve users in the ongoing maintenance of data quality. Encourage users to report issues, suggest improvements, and actively participate in data governance initiatives.

Compliance and Regulatory Alignment:

1. Understanding Regulatory Requirements:

- Stay informed about relevant data regulations and compliance requirements. Ensure that data governance practices within Power BI align with industry standards and legal obligations.

2. Data Audits and Compliance Checks:

- Conduct regular data audits and compliance checks. Evaluate data practices against established governance principles to identify and rectify any non-compliance issues.

Training and Awareness Programs:

1. Data Governance Training:

- Provide comprehensive training programs on data governance principles for Power BI users. Ensure that users are aware of their roles and responsibilities in maintaining data quality and security.

2. Continuous Awareness Initiatives:

- Implement continuous awareness initiatives, such as newsletters or training sessions, to keep Power BI users updated on evolving data governance practices and standards.

Implementing robust data governance principles in Power Query is instrumental in establishing a foundation of trust, accountability, and quality assurance within the Power BI environment. These principles contribute to a well-managed and compliant data ecosystem, promoting the effective use of data for business intelligence and decision-making.

11.3. Ensuring data security and compliance

Ensuring the security and compliance of data is paramount for any organization, especially in today's digital landscape where data breaches and regulatory requirements are prevalent. This section delves into the strategies and practices essential for safeguarding data integrity and maintaining regulatory compliance.

Understanding Data Security Measures

Before delving into specific security measures, it's crucial to comprehend the various aspects of data security. This includes understanding the sensitivity of different types of data, identifying potential vulnerabilities in data storage and transmission, and recognizing the importance of encryption, authentication, and access controls.

Data Classification:

- Sensitive Data Identification: Begin by identifying sensitive data within your organization, such as personally identifiable information (PII), financial records, or intellectual property. Classify data based on its sensitivity level to determine appropriate security measures.

- Data Mapping: Map out the flow of data within your organization, from its creation or acquisition to its storage, processing, and sharing. Understanding this flow helps identify potential security risks and implement effective controls.

Encryption and Data Masking:

- Encryption Protocols: Implement robust encryption protocols to protect data both at rest and in transit. Utilize encryption algorithms to encode sensitive information, rendering it unreadable to unauthorized users.

- Data Masking Techniques: Employ data masking techniques to obfuscate sensitive data when it's not necessary for users to view the actual values. This helps minimize the risk of data exposure during testing, development, or analytics processes.

Implementing Data Security Policies

Establishing comprehensive data security policies is essential for maintaining a secure environment. These policies outline the procedures, practices, and responsibilities related to data protection and compliance.

Access Controls:

- Role-Based Access Control (RBAC): Implement RBAC mechanisms to restrict access to data based on users' roles and responsibilities within the organization. Assign permissions and privileges in alignment with the principle of least privilege to minimize the risk of unauthorized access.

- Authentication Mechanisms: Implement strong authentication mechanisms, such as multi-factor authentication (MFA) or biometric authentication, to verify users' identities before granting access to sensitive data resources.

Data Loss Prevention (DLP):

- Monitoring and Auditing: Deploy monitoring and auditing tools to track data access, usage, and modifications. Regularly review audit logs to detect and investigate suspicious activities that may indicate potential data breaches or policy violations.

- Data Backup and Recovery: Establish robust data backup and recovery procedures to mitigate the impact of data loss incidents, whether caused by accidental deletion, hardware failure, or malicious attacks.

Ensuring Regulatory Compliance

Compliance with regulatory requirements is imperative for organizations operating in various industries, such as finance, healthcare, and telecommunications. Failure to comply with regulations can result in severe penalties and reputational damage.

Regulatory Frameworks:

- GDPR (General Data Protection Regulation): Ensure compliance with GDPR requirements, particularly regarding the processing and protection of personal data of EU citizens. Implement measures such as data anonymization, consent management, and data subject rights enforcement.

- HIPAA (Health Insurance Portability and Accountability Act): Adhere to HIPAA regulations if your organization handles protected health information (PHI). Implement safeguards to ensure the confidentiality, integrity, and availability of PHI, including access controls, encryption, and audit trails.

- PCI DSS (Payment Card Industry Data Security Standard): Comply with PCI DSS requirements if your organization processes payment card transactions. Implement measures to secure cardholder data, such as encryption, network segmentation, and regular vulnerability assessments.

Data Governance Frameworks:

- **Establishing Data Governance Committees:** Formulate data governance committees comprising stakeholders from various departments to oversee data security and compliance initiatives. These committees define policies, assess risks, and monitor adherence to regulatory requirements.

- **Continuous Compliance Monitoring:** Implement continuous compliance monitoring processes to ensure ongoing adherence to regulatory standards. Regularly assess and update security controls, conduct compliance audits, and provide staff training to maintain a culture of compliance within the organization.

Conclusion

Ensuring data security and compliance is an ongoing process that requires a combination of technical measures, robust policies, and organizational commitment. By implementing effective security controls, adhering to regulatory requirements, and fostering a culture of data stewardship, organizations can mitigate risks and safeguard their valuable assets from potential threats and regulatory scrutiny.

12. Performance Optimization

12.1. Optimizing queries for better performance

This section delves into the strategies and techniques for optimizing queries within Power Query, enhancing overall performance and ensuring efficient data processing.

Query Folding:

1. Understanding Query Folding:

- Explore the concept of query folding, where applicable. Query folding allows Power Query to push some data transformation operations back to the data source, optimizing performance by leveraging the capabilities of the underlying data engine.

2. Identifying Foldable Operations:

- Identify operations that support query folding, such as filtering and aggregation functions. Leveraging foldable operations can significantly reduce the amount of data transferred from the data source to Power Query.

Filtering and Reducing Data:

1. Applying Early Filtering:

- Implement early filtering by applying filters at the source level whenever possible. This reduces the volume of data retrieved, enhancing query performance by fetching only the necessary subset of records.

2. Removing Unnecessary Columns:

- Streamline queries by removing unnecessary columns early in the transformation process. This minimizes data size and speeds up subsequent operations.

Parameterizing Queries:

1. Dynamic Parameterization:

- Explore the use of parameters to create dynamic and reusable queries. Parameterizing queries allows for flexible data retrieval based on user inputs or changing requirements without compromising performance.

2. Utilizing Query Parameters:

- Incorporate query parameters for scenarios where users need to interact with the data, such as specifying date ranges or filtering criteria. This enables dynamic adjustments without the need for manual query modifications.

Optimizing Join Operations:

1. Choosing Efficient Join Types:

- Select appropriate join types based on the characteristics of the data. Inner joins are generally more efficient than outer joins, and choosing the right join strategy can significantly impact query performance.

2. Minimizing Join Complexity:

- Simplify join conditions and minimize the complexity of join operations. Complex join conditions can lead to performance bottlenecks, so ensure that join criteria are straightforward and well-defined.

Query Dependencies and Merging Steps:

1. Understanding Query Dependencies:

- Be mindful of the dependencies between different steps in a query. Understanding how each step contributes to the final result helps in optimizing the overall query structure.

2. Efficient Merging Techniques:

- Employ efficient merging techniques, especially when combining multiple tables. Utilize inner merges and leverage indexing strategies to enhance the speed of merging operations.

Limiting Data Preview and Loading:

1. Reducing Data Preview Size:

- Limit the size of data preview during query development. Loading large datasets for preview can consume resources unnecessarily, impacting performance during the development phase.

2. Partial Data Loading:

- Opt for partial data loading during query development if working with large datasets. Loading a subset of data facilitates faster query execution for testing and validation purposes.

Monitoring and Profiling:

1. Query Profiling Tools:

- Utilize query profiling tools within Power Query to identify performance bottlenecks. Profile queries to understand the execution plan and identify areas for optimization.

2. Monitoring Query Execution:

- Monitor query execution times and resource consumption. Keep an eye on performance metrics to detect deviations from expected performance levels and implement optimizations accordingly.

Documentation and Knowledge Sharing:

1. Best Practices Documentation:

- Document best practices for query optimization within the organization. Share this documentation with Power Query users to ensure a standardized approach to performance optimization.

2. Knowledge Sharing Sessions:

- Conduct knowledge-sharing sessions on query optimization techniques. Empower users with the skills to optimize their own queries, fostering a culture of continuous improvement.

By implementing these strategies, users can enhance the performance of their Power Query queries, leading to faster data transformations and improved overall efficiency in data processing workflows.

Example: Optimizing a Power Query for Better Performance

Consider a scenario where you have a large dataset containing sales transactions and customer information. The goal is to optimize a Power Query that merges two tables, filters data, and aggregates results.

Step 1: Early Filtering

- Original Query:

```
Source   =   Csv.Document(File.Contents("SalesData.csv"),[Delimiter=",",   Columns=4,
Encoding=65001, QuoteStyle=QuoteStyle.None]),

ConvertedTable   =   Table.TransformColumnTypes(Source,{{"Column1",   type   text},
{"Column2", type text}, {"Column3", type text}, {"Column4", type text}}),

MergedTables   =   Table.NestedJoin(ConvertedTable,   {"Column1"},   CustomerTable,
{"CustomerID"}, "CustomerInfo"),

ExpandedCustomerInfo   =   Table.ExpandTableColumn(MergedTables,   "CustomerInfo",
{"CustomerName", "City", "Country"}),

FilteredData = Table.SelectRows(ExpandedCustomerInfo, each [Country] = "USA"),

GroupedData   =   Table.Group(FilteredData,   {"CustomerID",   "CustomerName"},
{{"TotalSales", each List.Sum([Column3]), type number}}),
```

- Optimized Query:

```
Source   =   Csv.Document(File.Contents("SalesData.csv"),[Delimiter=",",   Columns=4,
Encoding=65001, QuoteStyle=QuoteStyle.None]),

ConvertedTable   =   Table.TransformColumnTypes(Source,{{"Column1",   type   text},
{"Column2", type text}, {"Column3", type text}, {"Column4", type text}}),

FilteredData = Table.SelectRows(ConvertedTable, each [Column4] = "USA"),

MergedTables   =   Table.NestedJoin(FilteredData,   {"Column1"},   CustomerTable,
{"CustomerID"}, "CustomerInfo"),

ExpandedCustomerInfo   =   Table.ExpandTableColumn(MergedTables,   "CustomerInfo",
{"CustomerName", "City", "Country"}),

GroupedData = Table.Group(ExpandedCustomerInfo, {"CustomerID", "CustomerName"},
{{"TotalSales", each List.Sum([Column3]), type number}}),
```

Step 2: Efficient Merging Techniques

- Original Query:

```
MergedTables    =    Table.NestedJoin(ConvertedTable,    {"Column1"},    CustomerTable,
{"CustomerID"}, "CustomerInfo"),
```

- Optimized Query:

```
MergedTables    =    Table.NestedJoin(FilteredData,    {"Column1"},    CustomerTable,
{"CustomerID"}, "CustomerInfo"),
```

Step 3: Parameterizing Queries

- Original Query:

```
FilteredData = Table.SelectRows(ExpandedCustomerInfo, each [Country] = "USA"),
```

- Optimized Query:

```
FilteredData = Table.SelectRows(ConvertedTable, each [Column4] = CountryParameter),
```

Step 4: Query Folding

- Original Query:

The original query may not fold certain operations back to the data source.

- Optimized Query:

Ensure that foldable operations are utilized where applicable, especially in filtering and aggregation steps.

Step 5: Monitoring and Profiling

- Query Profiling:

  - Utilize the "View Native Query" option in Power Query Editor to inspect whether certain operations are being folded back to the data source.

- Monitoring Query Execution:

  - Use the "Performance Analyzer" tool in Power BI to monitor query execution times and resource consumption.

Step 6: Documentation and Knowledge Sharing

- Best Practices Documentation:

  - Document the optimized query as a best practice example for users within the organization.

- Knowledge Sharing Sessions:

  - Conduct training sessions to share optimization techniques, emphasizing the importance of early filtering, efficient merging, parameterization, and query folding.

By applying these optimization steps, you can significantly enhance the performance of your Power Query, leading to faster data transformations and improved overall efficiency.

12.2. Troubleshooting slow queries and data refreshes

This section focuses on identifying and resolving issues related to slow queries and data refreshes in Power Query. Addressing performance issues is crucial for maintaining a responsive and efficient data processing environment.

Query Performance Monitoring:

1. Query Execution Times:

- Regularly monitor and log query execution times. Identify queries that take longer to execute, pinpointing potential bottlenecks in the data transformation process.

2. Resource Consumption Metrics:

- Use Power BI's built-in tools to measure resource consumption during query execution. Monitor CPU usage, memory consumption, and data transfer rates to detect patterns indicative of performance challenges.

Query Folding Verification:

1. Verifying Query Folding:

- Confirm whether query folding is occurring during data retrieval. Inspect the Power Query query execution plan to ensure that foldable operations are being pushed back to the data source for optimal performance.

2. Viewing Native Queries:

- Utilize the "View Native Query" feature in Power Query Editor to inspect the actual queries sent to the data source. This can help identify whether certain operations are being performed locally instead of at the source.

Data Source Connection and Refresh Optimization:

1. Connection Settings Review:

- Review and optimize the connection settings for data sources. Ensure that parameters such as timeouts and maximum rows are appropriately configured to avoid unnecessary delays.

2. Incremental Data Refresh:

- Implement incremental data refresh strategies where applicable. Rather than refreshing the entire dataset, selectively update only the new or modified data to reduce the refresh time.

Data Model Complexity Analysis:

1. Evaluating Data Model Complexity:

- Assess the complexity of the data model, especially if dealing with large datasets. Simplify relationships and calculations where possible to streamline data refresh operations.

2. Removing Unnecessary Steps:

- Identify and eliminate unnecessary steps in the Power Query transformation process. Reducing the number of transformations can lead to quicker query execution.

Parallel Loading and Refresh:

1. Parallel Loading Consideration:

- Explore options for parallel loading of data if supported by the data source. Parallel loading can enhance performance by fetching multiple datasets concurrently.

2. Optimizing Data Refresh Settings:

- Adjust data refresh settings to optimize parallel loading. Experiment with different settings to find the optimal configuration for your specific data source and requirements.

Cache Utilization and Memory Management:

1. Cache Utilization Review:

- Evaluate the usage of caching mechanisms during data refresh. Caching data locally can expedite query execution for subsequent refreshes.

2. Memory Management Settings:

- Adjust memory management settings in Power BI Desktop and Power BI Service. Allocating sufficient memory to Power Query operations can improve performance during data refresh.

Error Handling and Logging:

1. Error Handling Strategies:

- Implement robust error handling strategies within Power Query. Log and analyze errors to identify patterns and troubleshoot issues that may contribute to slow queries.

2. Logging Slow Queries:

- Implement logging mechanisms specifically for slow queries. Record details such as query text, execution time, and resource consumption to facilitate in-depth analysis.

Documentation and Knowledge Sharing:

1. Creating Troubleshooting Documentation:

- Develop troubleshooting documentation that guides users through identifying and resolving slow query issues. Include common scenarios and their solutions.

2. Sharing Troubleshooting Techniques:

- Conduct training sessions to share troubleshooting techniques with Power Query users. Empower users to proactively address performance issues during their data transformations.

By systematically addressing slow queries and data refresh challenges, users can optimize the performance of Power Query in their business intelligence workflows, ensuring timely and efficient data processing.

Example: Troubleshooting Slow Queries and Data Refreshes

Consider a scenario where you are working with a Power Query that loads sales data from a database. Over time, you notice that the data refresh is becoming slower. Let's troubleshoot and optimize the query.

Step 1: Query Performance Monitoring

1. Query Execution Times:

- In Power BI Desktop, open the Query Editor.

- Enable the "Diagnostic" option in the "View" tab to display query execution times.

- Execute the query and monitor the diagnostic information to identify the slowest steps.

2. Resource Consumption Metrics:

- Use the "Performance Analyzer" tool in Power BI to capture resource consumption metrics during query execution.

- Analyze CPU usage, memory consumption, and data transfer rates to identify resource-intensive steps.

Step 2: Query Folding Verification

1. Verifying Query Folding:

- In the Power Query Editor, right-click on a step and select "View Native Query" to inspect the native query sent to the data source.

- Confirm whether foldable operations are being utilized. Check for any non-foldable operations that might impact performance.

Step 3: Data Source Connection and Refresh Optimization

1. Connection Settings Review:

- In the Power Query Editor, navigate to the "Home" tab and select "Data Source Settings."

- Review and optimize connection settings, adjusting timeouts and other parameters as needed.

2. Incremental Data Refresh:

- If applicable, implement incremental data refresh.

- In the "Home" tab, go to "Transform Data," and use filtering or parameters to load only the new or modified data.

Step 4: Data Model Complexity Analysis

1. Evaluating Data Model Complexity:

- Review relationships and calculations in the data model.

- Simplify relationships where possible, and evaluate the necessity of complex calculations during data refresh.

2. Removing Unnecessary Steps:

- Identify and remove unnecessary steps in the query.

- Simplify transformations and focus on essential operations to reduce processing time.

Step 5: Parallel Loading and Refresh

1. Parallel Loading Consideration:

- Check if the data source supports parallel loading.

- Adjust the Power BI settings to enable parallel loading if beneficial.

2. Optimizing Data Refresh Settings:

- In Power BI Desktop, go to "File" -> "Options and settings" -> "Options."

- Navigate to the "Data Load" tab and adjust settings related to parallel loading.

Step 6: Cache Utilization and Memory Management

1. Cache Utilization Review:

- Check if caching is being utilized effectively.

- Experiment with caching settings to optimize data refresh.

2. Memory Management Settings:

- Adjust memory management settings in Power BI Desktop and Power BI Service to allocate sufficient memory for Power Query operations.

Step 7: Error Handling and Logging

1. Error Handling Strategies:

  - Review error handling strategies within the query.

  - Ensure that errors are logged and analyzed for patterns.

2. Logging Slow Queries:

  - Implement logging mechanisms specifically for slow queries.

  - Create a log that captures details such as query text, execution time, and resource consumption.

Step 8: Documentation and Knowledge Sharing

1. Creating Troubleshooting Documentation:

  - Document troubleshooting steps and best practices.

  - Share this documentation with other Power Query users within the organization.

2. Sharing Troubleshooting Techniques:

  - Conduct training sessions or workshops to share troubleshooting techniques with Power Query users.

  - Foster a collaborative environment for addressing performance issues.

By systematically following these steps and addressing specific issues identified during the troubleshooting process, users can optimize the performance of their Power Query, resulting in faster and more efficient data refreshes.

12.3. Best practices for efficient data manipulation

This section focuses on essential best practices for optimizing data manipulation in Power Query. Adhering to these practices enhances the efficiency and performance of data transformations, leading to a smoother business intelligence workflow.

1. Selectivity in Data Import:

- Apply filters or conditions during data import to bring in only the necessary rows or columns. This reduces the amount of data loaded into Power Query and speeds up the import process.

Example:

Source = Sql.Database("Server", "Database", [Query="SELECT FROM Sales WHERE Date >= '2022-01-01'"])

2. Use Query Folding:

- Leverage query folding whenever possible to push operations back to the data source. This ensures that transformations are performed at the source, minimizing data transfer and optimizing performance.

Example:

FilteredData = Table.SelectRows(Source, each [Category] = "Electronics")

3. Minimize Steps in Transformation:

- Keep the number of transformation steps to a minimum. Each step adds processing overhead, so streamline transformations by combining or eliminating unnecessary operations.

Example:

// Unnecessary step

RemovedColumns = Table.RemoveColumns(FilterRows, {"UnusedColumn"})

// Streamlined version

FilteredData = Table.SelectColumns(Source, {"Column1", "Column2", "Column3"})

4. Parameterize Queries:

- Parameterize queries to make them more flexible and reusable. This allows users to adjust query behavior without modifying the query code, facilitating efficient data manipulation across different scenarios.

Example:

// Parameterized query

DateParameter = #datetime(2022, 1, 1, 0, 0, 0),

FilteredData = Table.SelectRows(Source, each [Date] >= DateParameter)

5. Indexing for Large Tables:

- Create indexes on columns used for filtering and joining, especially in large tables. Indexing accelerates data retrieval, improving the performance of operations that involve these columns.

Example:

// Creating an index

IndexedTable = Table.AddIndexColumn(Source, "RowIndex", 1, 1, Int64.Type)

6. Avoid Unnecessary Calculations:

- Minimize unnecessary calculations during data transformation. Evaluate and remove any calculations that do not contribute to the final result, reducing processing time.

Example:

// Unnecessary calculation

AddedColumn = Table.AddColumn(Source, "UnusedColumn", each [Column1] [Column2])

// Revised version

RemovedColumn = Table.RemoveColumns(Source, {"UnusedColumn"})

7. Optimize Memory Usage:

- Be mindful of memory consumption, especially when dealing with large datasets. Use the "Remove Other Columns" option to retain only essential columns, reducing the memory footprint of the query.

Example:

// Retaining only essential columns

ReducedMemoryData = Table.SelectColumns(Source, {"Column1", "Column2", "Column3"})

8. Use Native Functions:

- Prefer native functions and operations provided by Power Query over custom functions. Native functions are optimized for performance and can lead to faster data manipulation.

Example:

// Native function for filtering

FilteredData = Table.SelectRows(Source, each [Category] = "Electronics")

// Custom function (less efficient)

FilteredData = MyCustomFilterFunction(Source, "Electronics")

9. Apply Query Folding in Custom Functions:

- When creating custom functions, ensure they support query folding. This allows Power Query to push operations performed in the custom function back to the data source.

Example:

// Query-folding-friendly custom function

(dataSource, filterValue) =>

  let

    FilteredData = Table.SelectRows(dataSource, each [Category] = filterValue)

  in

    FilteredData

10. Document Transformation Logic:

- Document the logic of complex transformations within the query. Use comments and annotations to explain the purpose of each step, making it easier for others to understand and maintain the code.

Example:

// Extracting year from the Date column

YearColumn = Table.AddColumn(Source, "Year", each Date.Year([Date]))

By incorporating these best practices into your data manipulation workflows, you can optimize Power Query performance and ensure efficient handling of diverse datasets in your business intelligence projects.

Conclusion

In concluding this journey through "Power Query for Business Intelligence: A Beginner's Guide," we trust that you have gained a solid foundation in harnessing the power of Power Query for effective data manipulation, analysis, and reporting. The book has been designed to equip beginners with the essential skills needed to navigate the intricate landscape of business intelligence, providing practical insights and hands-on experience in leveraging Power Query for diverse tasks.

Throughout the chapters, you have explored key concepts such as data modeling, aggregation, M Language, business intelligence principles, and more. Each section has been crafted to offer a step-by-step approach, ensuring that you not only understand the theoretical aspects but also gain a hands-on understanding of applying these concepts in real-world scenarios.

As you embark on your business intelligence journey, remember that continuous learning and exploration are vital. Power Query is a dynamic tool, and as your understanding deepens, you'll discover new ways to extract valuable insights from your data, making informed decisions for your organization.

We encourage you to continue practicing and experimenting with Power Query, incorporating the knowledge gained from this guide into your daily workflows. Whether you are a business analyst, data professional, or anyone eager to unlock the potential of your data, the skills acquired here will serve as a valuable asset in your professional toolkit.

Acknowledgments:

We extend our heartfelt gratitude to you, dear reader, for choosing "Power Query for Business Intelligence: A Beginner's Guide" as your companion on this learning journey. Your curiosity and dedication to mastering Power Query are commendable, and we sincerely hope that the knowledge imparted in these pages proves invaluable to your endeavors.

Special thanks to our dedicated team, whose collective efforts and commitment have brought this book to fruition. From concept to completion, each contributor played a crucial role in ensuring the clarity, accuracy, and practicality of the content.

Remember, the world of business intelligence is ever-evolving, and your understanding of Power Query positions you at the forefront of this transformative field. May your data explorations be insightful, and your analytical endeavors yield meaningful results.

Wishing you continued success and fulfillment in your data-driven endeavors!

www.ingramcontent.com/pod-product-compliance
Lightning Source LLC
LaVergne TN
LVHW081345050326
832903LV00024B/1333